Invoice Verification for SAP

Stephen Birchall

Contents

Preface 5
    Acknowledgments 5

1 What is Invoice Verification? 7
1.1 High-Level Process 7
    The Main Steps 7
    Capturing the Invoice Details 8
    The Use of Invoice Verification 9
    Processing Mismatched Invoices 10
1.2 Handling Mismatched Invoices 11
    Mismatches During Input (MIRO) ... 11
1.3 Processing Blocked Invoices 12
    Using Workflow when Mismatches Occur 13
    Using Transaction MRBR 14
    Automatic Invoice Release 14
1.4 Parking Invoices 15
1.5 Workflow in Invoice Verification 16
1.6 Summary 17

2 Specific Functions in Detail 19
2.1 The Goods Receipt-Based Invoice Verification (GR-Based IV) Flag 19
    What Does the GR-Based IV Flag Do? ... 19
    The Risks of Setting the Flag Off 20
    The Risks of Setting the Flag On 20
    On Vs. Off 21
    How the Flag Works 21
    Entering an Invoice for a Purchase Order with the Flag Set On 22
    Entering an Invoice for a Purchase Order with the Flag Set Off 23
    Where is the Flag Set? 23

2.2 Delivery Charges (Planned and Unplanned) ... 24
    Difference Between Planned and Unplanned Delivery Charges 24
    A Third Option 24
    Planned Delivery Charges 25
    Posting Planned Delivery Charges in Invoice Verification 27
    Unplanned Delivery Charges 28
    A Third Option 28
2.3 Tolerances 29
    Why Have Tolerances? 29
    What Kind of Tolerances are There? ... 29
    Special Tolerances 29
    Other Tolerances 30
    Configuring the Tolerances 30
    Error Messages Resulting from Tolerances 30
2.4 Evaluated Receipt Settlement (ERS) ... 31
    How Does ERS Work? 31
    How Safe is the Process? 31
    ERS for Inter- or Intra-Company Scenarios 31
    The ERS Process 31
    The ERS Settlement Transaction 32
2.5 Invoice Reduction 33
    What Does Invoice Reduction Do? ... 33
    The Invoice-Reduction Process 33
    The Financial Posting of the Difference ... 35
2.6 Pipeline and Consignment Stock Settlement 35
    Consignment Stock 35
    Pipeline Stock 36
2.7 Invoicing Plans 36
    Periodic Invoicing Plans 37

www.sap-press.com   1

Contents

	Partial Invoicing Plans 37			Running F110 59
	How Does the Process Work? 38			The F110S Transaction 59
	Invoice Verification Relating to		3.7	Summary 60
	Invoicing Plans 39			
	Basic Configuration for Invoicing Plans ... 39		**4**	**Configuration** **61**
2.8	Subsequent Debits and Credits 39		4.1	Basic Configuration 61
	Posting a Subsequent Credit 39		4.2	Define the Attributes of System Messages 62
	Posting a Subsequent Debit 40			How to Configure System Messages 63
	Posting a Normal Credit 40		4.3	Define Tax Jurisdiction 64
2.9	Purchase Order Texts 40		4.4	Configure Automatic Postings 65
	The Basic Process 41			Account Assignment 65
	An Example of How to Use this			Simulation 68
	Function 41			G/L Accounts Function 70
2.10	New Functionality in Release ERP 6.0 42		4.5	Incoming Invoice 70
	ERS for Delivery Charges 42			Number Assignment 70
	Prepayment of Invoices 43			Tax Treatment in Invoice Reduction 71
	Variance Types 44			Maintain Default Values for Tax Codes 71
	Assignment Test 44			Configure Treatment of Exchange-Rate
	Other New Functions and Options now			Differences 72
	Available 45			Configure Posting of Unplanned
2.11	Summary 47			Delivery Costs 72
				Edit PO Supplement Text in
3	**Financial Aspects of Invoice Verification** **49**			Invoice Verification 72
3.1	Overview 49			Define Mail to Purchasing When Price
3.2	Automatic Account Determination 49			Variances Occur 73
3.3	The Goods-Received/Invoice-Received			Configure Vendor-Specific Tolerances 73
	Clearing Account 50			Maintain Bar-Code Entry 73
	Sample Scenarios for the Use of the			Activate Direct Posting to G/L Accounts
	GR/IR Clearing Account 50			and Material Account 73
	Using MR11 to Manage the GR/IR			Maintain Item-List Variants 74
	Clearing Account 51			Aggregation 74
	Regular Maintenance of the Clearing			Define Start Logo 74
	Accounts 53			Set Check for Duplicate Invoices 74
3.4	Tax Processing Within Invoice Verification 54			Nota Fiscal and Chain Liabilities 75
	The Calculate Tax Flag 55			Prepayment (New to ERP 6) 75
	The Tax Tab in the MIRO Transaction 55			Variance types (New to ERP 6) 76
3.5	Moving Average Price/Standard Price 55			Assignment Test (New to ERP 6) 77
	The Difference Between Standard Pricing		4.6	Document Parking 78
	and MAP 56		4.7	Invoice Block 78
	Advantages of Each Option 56			Determine Payment Block 78
3.6	Payment Run 57			Set Tolerance Limits 78
	Parameter Tab 57			Activate Workflow Template 81
	The Free Selection Tab 58			Item Amount Check 81
	The Additional Log tab 58			Stochastic Blocks 81
	The Printout/Data Medium Tab 59		4.8	Clearing Account Maintenance 82

4.9	Invoice Verification in Background	82
4.10	Electronic Data Interchange (EDI)	82
4.11	Evaluated Release Settlement (ERS)	82
	Specify Automatic Settlement of Planned Delivery Costs (New to ERP 6)	82
	ERS Invoice Numbering (New to ERP 6)	83
4.12	Message Determination	83
4.13	Define Document Life	83
4.14	Authorization Management	83
4.15	Maintain Customer Exits and Business Add-Ins	83
4.16	Logistics Invoice Verification: Index	83
4.17	Business Add-Ins and User Exits in Invoice Verification (New to ERP 6)	84
	Changes to Existing User Exits and Includes in Latest Releases	84
4.18	Summary	85
	Index	87

Preface

The invoice verification process within SAP suffers from the fact that it appears to be strictly an SAP Financials function and yet it is located in the Materials Management (MM) menus and configuration. In most implementations, the task of designing the process and configuring the functionality is given to the Financials team, but in some it is given to the MM team. In fact, both approaches are likely to result in a less — than — efficient process because invoice verification is one of the few tasks that has to be managed by both teams working together.

When the functionality and processes have been designed with full involvement from both teams, success is more likely, though even then it depends on the basic understanding of the process. Too often, the standard SAP functionality is misunderstood and the resulting process is far from efficient.

The overused recommendation to "keep it simple" applies absolutely to SAP Invoice Verification. Consider that the task of entering an invoice into the system adds little value to a business, especially given that you already know how much the vendor is entitled to from the purchase order and receipt details and so could simply send a payment without even entering an invoice. We are not suggesting that you simply switch to Evaluated Receipt Settlement (ERS) — sometimes referred to as self-billing — but you should realize that this is possible. If your invoice verification process is in any way complicated or uses a lot of resources, you may benefit from looking at the process from a completely different angle.

This book will explain the processes provided by SAP and show how you can keep the whole function standardized and simple without losing any vital functionality. The end result should be a process that flows well and is seen to be efficient and accurate. Some functions should be avoided and others should be embraced, and the reasons for this will be explained along with the detailed information you need to configure the invoice verification function correctly.

Whether you are about to implement the SAP Invoice Verification function or have already done so, you will find this book informative, even if you don't believe you are having any problems with the functionality.

The book covers the functionality that is relevant for releases up to and including ERP6 (also known as ERP 2005 and ECC5 and ECC6).

Acknowledgments

This book is dedicated to my grandchildren: Stephen, Harvey, Rupinder, Balvinder, George, and Joseph. To my precious wife Joan, and to all of our children, who constantly make me so glad to be a part of their lives. And to all of my colleagues, who have endured my terrible sense of humor.

1 What is Invoice Verification?

Most organizations that struggle with poor implementations of SAP Invoice Verification misunderstand the basic process involved. Invoice Verification is simply a function that allows you to capture the details of vendor invoices. If you start from this admittedly simplified viewpoint, the basic design will more likely be robust and you will be more likely to have a process that works as it should.

Having said that, it is merely a method of capturing the details from the vendor's invoice, it's clear that the function does a lot more than this, but you can deal with the remainder of the design once you have established the basic principle. For instance, if the details of the invoice that was captured in this way match the expected details specified by any related purchase order (PO) and goods receipt (GR), the invoice can be made available automatically for payment. Unmatched invoices are excluded from the payment run and need to be investigated and released before payments can be made. If you make this basic process overly complex or inefficient (by straying too far from the basic SAP functionality), payments made to vendors will be late. Possible consequences of this include a loss of cash discounts, having purchase orders rejected by the vendor, and even losing the vendor account.

It is essential, therefore, to understand the basic process of invoice verification before you design or modify it. It is equally important to have confidence in the SAP standard functionality, even though it may appear to be very different from your current processes. The standard process provided by SAP is suitable for most businesses, though this may not appear to be the case at first glance. The standard process has many configuration options and is normally more than flexible enough to cater to the needs of an invoice verification department, be that a global "shared service center" or a local accounts-payable department.

Because you are most likely to succeed if you adopt the standard SAP process, rather than trying to alter the SAP process to fit your current functionality, we will start with a high-level view of the process.

1.1 High-Level Process

The main aim of any invoice verification process is to ensure that vendors are paid the correct amount at the right time (not too late but also not too early). The process should have a high incidence of first-time matching to ensure that as little time as possible is spent trying to manually match invoices that appear to be incorrect. It is important to include as few steps as possible in the process, considering that the process of handling payments does not in itself add value to the company.

The Main Steps

The main steps included in the process are:
- Capture of the vendor's invoice details
- Matching of those details to the details that we believe to be correct
- Investigation and management of any mismatches
- Release for payment of validated invoices
- Accounting entries (including taxes and delivery costs)
- Details recorded for audit purposes

It is important to keep these steps to a minimum and the SAP processes achieve this goal. Additional steps are counter-productive and add little or no additional value, so please do not add extra steps or functions unless they are absolutely required.

The capture and matching of the invoice occurs in one transaction (transaction MIRO). A payment block is set if

1 What is Invoice Verification?

Figure 1.1 Main MIRO Transaction Screen

the match is unsuccessful. Figure 1.1 shows the main screen of the MIRO transaction.

If an invoice has been blocked during invoice verification, transaction MRBR must be used to manage the blocks on that invoice. Some organizations remove the blocks using other transactions and this must not be done. This will interfere with the data that MRBR uses and can show the invoice as blocked in MRBR but allowed through the payment run. Try to retain the full standard SAP process, which includes MRBR as a critical transaction. Figure 1.2 shows the main selection screen of the MRBR transaction.

The accounting entries are updated when the values are posted (in both transactions), as are the records of events for audit or inquiry purposes. These two transactions are the main steps involved. The only other transactions needed to manage the process are inquiry or cancellation transactions. If you have built your process to include more steps than this, you may be adding extra complexity for little or no extra value.

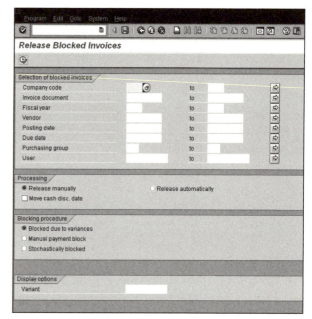

Figure 1.2 Main MRBR Transaction Selection Screen

Capturing the Invoice Details

This step uses transaction MIRO and is the main step in the process. Remember that this transaction is simply designed to capture the details from the vendor's invoice

8 © Galileo Press 2008. All rights reserved.

1.1 High-Level Process

Figure 1.3 Sample Completed MIRO Screen

and so you must focus on that process. If the details entered from the vendor's invoice match the details (quantity and value) of what the system believes to be owed to the vendor (based on the PO and the GR), this transaction completes the process and passes the details to the payment run. This ensures that the vendor is paid the correct amount at the appropriate time (considering the payment terms that apply). No further steps are required if the invoice matches here, apart from the scheduled payment runs. While this is a very important transaction, it does not need to be carried out by senior financial staff. The person entering the data is merely entering the vendor's invoice values and quantities so that the system can determine of the payment should be made.

The Use of Invoice Verification
This transaction is designed to be used by any member of the financial staff, however junior that person may be. It is designed so that the minimum amount of data needs to be entered. For instance, when the PO number has been specified, the system will calculate the balance owing to the vendor based on the PO prices, the GRs that have been processed, and any invoices already posted for this PO. It will then propose those values on the screen. If they match the values on the invoice being processed, the invoice can be posted by saving the transaction. Figure 1.3 shows the MIRO main screen with the details completed.

The system will use the details entered (or left as proposed) to attempt a match against what we believe the vendor is entitled to; only if this matches will a payment be proposed. Figure 1.4 shows the traffic-light icon and zero-balance that indicate that the invoice match is successful. A green traffic-light icon means that a match has been made and no payment block will be used. Amber means that the invoice details add up correctly but do not match the details expected for that invoice and a payment block will be applied. Red means that the invoice cannot be posted because the total amount on the invoice differs from the sum of the invoice lines entered.

Figure 1.4 Traffic-Light Icon and Zero-Balance Indicating Successful Invoice Match

www.sap-press.com 9

Some people assume that the reason that only certain-finance staff should use this transaction is because the operator can change details on the screen to match the details on the vendor's invoice. This occurs when the operator is entering the details and the vendor is asking for more (or less) than the amount proposed by the system. This results in a red traffic-light, and no posting can be made until the details are changed. The reason for this is that the system is indicating that the total invoice value does not match the sum of the invoice lines being processed. This is often because the system defaulted the line-level data, but the invoice lines from the vendor contain data different from this.

The remedy is to change the invoice-line data in MIRO to match the invoice-line data. At first, this may seem to involve risk. But if you remember that this transaction is really just capturing the details from the vendor's invoice, then you realize that changing the details does not actually authorize any payment; it is merely indicating the data that the vendor has included on the invoice, however correct (or incorrect) that is. In fact, this transaction doesn't even require human input; it can be carried out using scanning equipment and appropriate software (in fact several organizations already use this method to enter invoices into SAP). Think of this process as a method of simply capturing the invoice details, with the rest happening automatically. If the invoice matches, then it is passed for payment. If it does not match, the details are still captured but the payment is blocked and so the person entering the data cannot make the system pay an amount greater than the vendor is entitled to.

Processing Mismatched Invoices

The standard SAP method (and in our view, the only method to adopt) of managing mismatched or blocked invoices is to use transaction MRBR.

Mismatched invoices are those where the details on the invoice do not match the details expected based on the PO. Blocked invoices include those that have been blocked because of other tolerances, such as the invoice being sent in too early.

This transaction lists all of the invoices that have been blocked for payment. It gives details of what is blocked, what value or quantity is involved, why it has been blocked, when, and by whom. Figure 1.5 shows a typical list of mismatched invoices displayed using transaction MRBR.

If investigation shows the vendor's details were correct, the details of the PO or GR should be corrected so that the invoice details match. The next MRBR run that has been selected to automatically release invoices will then release these for payment. MRBR will automatically release an invoice for payment once the reasons for the block are no longer valid, but only if you schedule MRBR as a regular job with the "automatic release" option set.

If investigations show that the blocks are still valid — that is, if we disagree with the vendor's details — then the invoice can remain blocked for as long as required or until a credit note has been posted for the relevant PO. If, in certain unusual circumstances, the vendor's invoice details are correct but we cannot change the PO or goods-receipt details to ensure a match, we can use MRBR to remove blocks manually and release invoices even though they do not match. For this reason, MRBR is a transaction that must be limited to authorized users in the business. These must be users with authority to write a company check, as they are effectively paying a vendor something that we have indicated that we do not owe them.

Doc. no.	Year	Type	Posting Date	Inv. pty	Bline date	Invitem	Amount	Purch.Doc	Item	Quantity	OUn	SD	Opq	Qty	Prc	Qua	ItA	Dte	Man	Difference Quantity	Difference value
510564...	2005	RE	15.09.2005	1005...	31.08.2005	3	171.99	4500041...	30	1.000	IT			X						0	17.20
510565...	2005	RE	22.11.2005	1039...	18.09.2005	22	1,900.00	4500038...	230	5.000	D		X							5	0.00
510565...	2005	RE	13.12.2005	1039...	05.12.2005	26	1,750.00	4500038...	260	5.000	D		X							5	0.00
510566...	2006	RE	07.02.2006	1002...	16.11.2004	1	245.00	4500050...	10	1.000	EA		X							1	0.00

Figure 1.5 MRBR List Screen Showing Mismatched Invoices

1.2 Handling Mismatched Invoices

There are primarily two situations in which you have to deal with mismatched invoices. These are:
- During input (in MIRO)
- After the input of the invoice

Mismatches During Input (MIRO)

The MIRO transaction performs two main checks, and it is vital to understand the difference between these two checks, especially in the ways that they affect the ability to post the invoice. These are as follows:
- The first check ensures that the details entered add up mathematically (i.e., the invoice value matches the sum of the invoice lines entered or proposed by the system).
- The second checks to see if the invoice should be blocked or made available for payment.

Tolerances do not affect the first check because, after all, a mathematical check is not meant to deliver *approximate* results. Having said this, there is one exception: a tolerance known as the *manage-small-differences tolerance*. This is designed to control the rounding errors (mainly during tax calculations, etc.). If the documents mathematically match within the configured tolerance, the system can then accept this as a rounding error and allow the process to continue to the next stage where the remainder of the invoice tolerances can be checked. Make sure that this tolerance (covered in more detail in later chapters) is switched on and is only set to very small amounts.

The second check relies on the majority of the configurable invoice tolerances. If the invoice passes the first check, (i.e., it therefore adds up mathematically) it can be posted. The remainder of the tolerances are then checked to see if the payment block needs to be set.

When posting an invoice with reference to a PO or similar, the system will fill in most of the data for you, apart from the invoice value, including the value of the vendor's invoice including all taxes and discounts. The data is taken from the PO referenced in the PO field on the main screen of transaction MIRO and the GRs that have been posted against this PO and not yet invoiced. The actual invoice data is being presented by the vendor, and thus the data proposed by the system may not match the data from the vendor's invoice. This means that when the system adds up the line items and compares the result against the total value you manually entered in the **Amount** field of the **Basic data** tab, it may not add up mathematically. The system therefore prevents the posting of the invoice simply because the total value you keyed does not match the total of all of the invoice lines.

To post the invoice, you must make sure that the value of the line items adds up to the total value of the invoice as keyed into the **Amount** field value (with taxes considered). If the values do not add up, you will have to check each line on the vendor's invoice against the data proposed by the system and correct any differences by changing the line data on the screen. You are not changing the amount that the vendor will be paid or authorizing any changes in values or quantities; you are merely entering the data as it appears on the invoice. This is exactly the same data that you would have had to manually enter line by line if the system did not propose these values for you. So you should think of the system proposed values as being there purely to help to reduce the keying that is required, which it actually achieves if the proposed values are correct, as they often are.

Figure 1.6 shows the MIRO main screen with the **Amount** field entered and the line details proposed by the system, based on data taken from the referenced purchase order.

This is where some people mistakenly get the idea that changing these values is somehow authorizing the payment. In reality, it simply ensures that the system knows the details of the invoice so that a match can be attempted. Changing these values does not authorize payment but merely indicates what the vendor is asking for on the invoice.

The second check that is carried out is where the main invoice tolerances play a part. If any differences are identified during this check and they are within the tolerances, then the invoice is posted and the payment is not blocked. If not, the invoice can still be posted (subject to other conditions covered in later chapters) but the payment will be blocked.

Invoice tolerances really only control whether the payment is to be blocked; they do not control whether the invoice can be posted (apart from the rounding tolerance, i.e., small differences).

1 What is Invoice Verification?

Figure 1.6 MIRO Screen Showing Data Obtained from Referenced Purchase Order

Figure 1.7 shows an invoice that does not balance mathematically. The invoice total is 2,350 and the value-added tax (VAT) is 350, but the value from the PO (price multiplied by un-invoiced receipts) does not add up to this value. Therefore, the invoice cannot be posted because of this mathematical discrepancy.

1.3 Processing Blocked Invoices

When an invoice has been blocked for payment because of a mismatch that is outside the invoice tolerances, the only difference between this invoice and an invoice that has not been blocked for payment is the setting of the payment-blocking flags. The financial postings are the

Figure 1.7 Invoice Failing Mathematical Check

same, including display of the invoice as an open item on the vendor account and posting of any price variances to the appropriate accounts, etc. This is because the invoice is the latest communication from the vendor relating to these items and so the data on that invoice is assumed to be accurate until determined otherwise.

Figure 1.8 shows an invoice with a payment-blocking flag. In this case an R flag has been automatically set to indicate an invoice verification block.

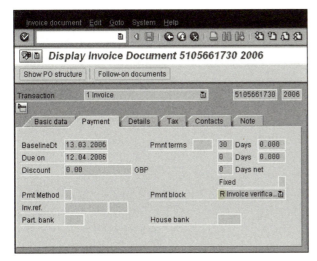

Figure 1.8 Payment-Blocking Flag

The only action needed to process blocked invoices is to decide if the blocks should be removed. There are two correct ways to remove the payment blocks blocks, both using transaction MRBR. These are:

- Manually within MRBR, by indicating which block or blocks are to be removed
- Automatically, by running MRBR with the automatic release flag set on

Many people make the mistake of simply removing the blocks using a Financials transaction such as FBL1N. This removes the flag and allows a payment to be made, but it does not process the blocked record properly, so the items still appear in the blocked invoice transaction (MRBR) even after they have been released.

Figure 1.9 shows the FBL1N screen that should not be used to manually release invoices.

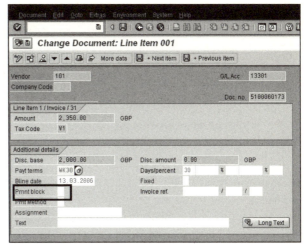

Figure 1.9 Initial FBL1N Transaction Screen

Caution: Only use MRBR to process blocked invoices. Removing the payment block via any other transaction can result in corrupting the data that MRBR uses.

Using Workflow when Mismatches Occur

When an invoice is blocked during MIRO — due to a quantity or value mismatch or some other factor — someone will have to investigate the problem and decide the action to take, but how are they informed that there is a problem and what caused it? Many organizations simply photocopy the invoice and pass it to the appropriate department with a handwritten explanation of the problem. This works well enough if the volumes of invoices that are posted are low and only a few people are involved in the investigations. This keeps it simple and can often the best way to handle this situation.

However, if the volumes are large or many people are involved in the investigations, then a more sophisticated solution is required. This is where a standard SAP workflow function plays a very useful part in the process. Transaction MIRO can trigger a workflow message (normally a SAPmail or email message that can be formatted to suit your needs) to an appropriate user — for example, the person who raised the PO or the purchasing group responsible for that PO — whenever a mismatch occurs. This is normally a request to check or correct a price or to complete a GR that has not yet been keyed.

www.sap-press.com   13

1 What is Invoice Verification?

The usual response to these messages is to carry out the change to the PO or to post the GR (If the invoice details are correct) or to reply stating that the PO and GR details are correct and the vendor's invoice should not be paid yet.

This is a standard option in SAP and requires minimal configuration and setup, especially if you have access to a workflow consultant.

Using Transaction MRBR

Transaction MRBR should be checked regularly (ideally at least once a day), and this transaction should be seen as the sole transaction for managing blocked invoices. You can list blocked invoices by vendor, by date, by purchasing group, or by user, among other criteria and therefore it is easy enough to create a meaningful list of the problem invoices. By creating this list you can see invoices that have been blocked for some time and ensure that these are acted on before the vendor starts to take action. The system will display the blocked invoices that match the selection options, and you will then be able to release invoices or remove blocking reasons, manually if required.

Figure 1.10 shows an example of the screen used to manually manage blocked invoices.

Manual release of an invoice or removal of a blocking reason should only be necessary when you do not wish to change the purchase order to correct the price or when you wish to pay for the items even though a receipt may not be have been fully posted. This might occur when the vendor's invoice is correct and for whatever reason you do not want to change the error on the PO or to post the remaining GR. This should be a very rare occurrence and should not be part of the normal invoice-management process. To release an invoice manually, you can either select individual blocking reasons (quantity, price, date, etc.) and remove the block, or simply release the whole invoice.

It is recommended that wherever possible the PO price and GRs be corrected. The next run of the automatic release of blocked invoices (via MRBR) would then release these invoices once the reason for the blocks is no longer valid.

Note: You cannot release part of an invoice for payment. The invoice is either blocked or available for payment in total.

Automatic Invoice Release

In reality there is no automatic invoice release for payment, as such. If you have an invoice that was blocked because the GR has not yet been posted and then the GR is posted, the invoice will not be automatically released for payment. But you can use transaction MRBR in a scheduled job with the flag **Release automatically** set on, and this will then release all invoices where the blocking reason is no longer relevant. This will perform the same way as an automatic release, but will only release when the job has run. Ideally, this should be at least once a day. Figure 1.11 shows the position of the flag on the initial screen of transaction MRBR to indicate that an automatic release is to be carried out.

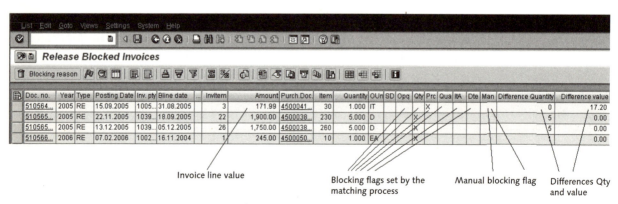

Figure 1.10 Mismatched Invoices Displayed Within Transaction MRBR

Figure 1.11 Release Automatically Flag in MRBR Initial Screen

1.4 Parking Invoices

Be careful with this function because it has a very specific use and it is not designed to be part of the core process of posting invoices. Many implementations use this function as a step that every invoice goes through. While this can be done, bear in mind that this is not what the parking function was designed for and so you may find that it does not actually do exactly what you would expect. The invoice-parking functionality provided by SAP has a very specific purpose, and if you are using it for this purpose then it functions well. If, on the other hand, you are using the parking process as a specific step in the normal processing of invoices, then you may find that it is not adding value to the process and may be adding complexity that is not required.

The function has been provided to address situations where the user does not wish to complete the invoice verification transaction but wishes to keep the data that has been entered. This is ideal if a complex invoice is being processed and there is not enough time to complete the transaction. The data entered so far can be parked and returned to at a later stage.

There are two main ways to park an invoice. The most common is to decide while posting an invoice that you wish to exit and save your work without processing the invoice. To do this, you can use the menu option **Edit • Switch to Document Parking**. This will allow you to save the work you have done so far without the document being posted.

The other option is to start off by using the invoice-parking function directly, instead of MIRO, using transaction MIR7. This is used in situations where you know that you will not want to process the invoice at this stage. Figure 1.12 shows the initial screen of the MIR7 invoice-parking transaction. Note how similar this is to the MIRO screen.

This is where some implementations misuse the function. Sometimes people interpret the invoice-parking function as an integral step in the process. It appears that all invoices could be posted as parked first, and then someone else (perhaps someone more senior) could process the parked invoice into a fully processed invoice. This can be done, and we have seen it used in this way in some implementations, but you have to bear in mind that it was not designed to be used in this way and so is unlikely to function in the way you hoped. In the implementations we have seen, parking was excessive because of overuse of the GR-based invoice verification flag (covered in detail in Section 2.1) and a combination of the misuse of both of these functions (parking and the GR-based IV flag) can lead to serious problems, especially in the GR/IR clearing account.

For instance, you can view and monitor parked invoices using transaction MIR6, the invoice-overview function, but there is no ideal transaction that ensures that all parked documents are processed in a timely fash-

1   What is Invoice Verification?

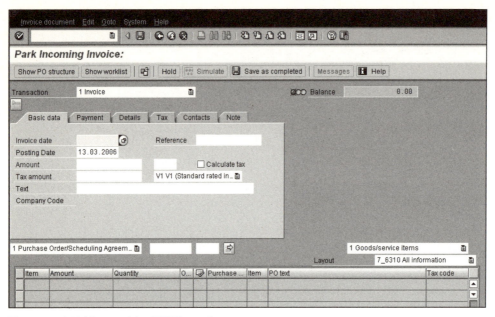

Figure 1.12   Initial Screen of the MIR7 Transaction

ion. This can result in some invoices being overlooked or, worse still, duplicated. This is not a failing of the SAP system, but occurs because this is not the main purpose of the parking function.

Figure 1.13 shows you how to view or manage parked invoices with transaction MIR6.

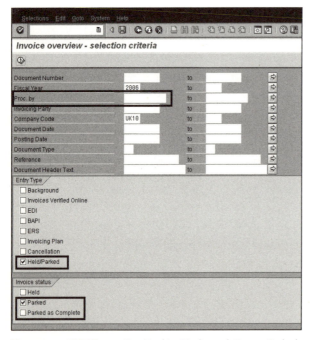

Figure 1.13   MIR6 Transaction Used to Display and Manage Parked Invoices

Some implementations then tie in workflow functions to manage the processing of parked invoices, and this adds even more complexity (and little true added value).

However, if the whole invoice verification function is fully understood, then you are unlikely to find any benefit from using it in this way. The incorrect use of the GR-based invoice verification flag often makes it necessary to park far more invoices than necessary. This is another subject covered in later chapters.

1.5   Workflow in Invoice Verification

Workflow is a very useful tool within SAP. Some people describe it as event-triggered messaging, but we prefer to refer to it as event-triggered events. Basically, you can use workflow to send a message when an event occurs, or you can trigger an action or another transaction when an event occurs.

The workflow function can be used throughout the SAP functionality and is not restricted to certain events or transactions. However, you will find that in some standard transactions SAP has integrated basic workflow functionality. Invoice verification is one example of this. SAP has a pre-defined workflow template — WS20000397 — specifically for the management of mismatched invoices.

The standard workflow function in invoice verification is designed to be used to send a workflow message via email or SAPmail to a user. There is no specific layout for this message; you can word and format it as required. The user would be informed that the invoice did not match and be told if the mismatch resulted from a price or quantity variance. Full details of the purchase order can be included in the message, and further processing can be carried out within the message. For example, you could go to the purchase order change function or the goods-receipt function directly from within the message.

This function can be very useful when several people are responsible for POs and GRs. If only a few users are involved in your PO processing, then it may be easier to just send a photocopy of the invoice in the internal post with the details of the problem.

The workflow process can be configured to use various methods of determining to whom the message should be sent. It could be the user who created the PO, the requisitioner, or the person responsible for posting GRs at the plant or storage location on the PO. If there are complicated rules to be followed, then this can be achieved by basic Advanced Business Application Programming (ABAP) coding. ABAP is SAP's programming language.

All in all, the workflow function is very useful. It should be considered as not only a user-friendly function, but also as a good way to ensure that mismatches are handled quickly and by the appropriate person, without the possibility of omissions due to lost paperwork or other issues.

As for developing workflow solutions in other areas of invoice verification, or anywhere else in SAP, we have a word of warning. The functionality offered by workflow can dramatically improve many processes, and it can be used to make the system capable of other very useful functions. It does have an overhead, however, and that is the technical maintenance. This is a small price to pay for the many benefits that can be achieved, but it has to be considered fully when determining if workflow is appropriate.

It is possible for workflow records to occasionally have technical problems, and this may result in the message not being received or processed by the user. This will leave an unprocessed record that has to be resolved by someone with workflow skills. If you multiply this possibility by the number of messages that are transmitted, then this problem resolution can become almost a full-time task.

Other problems, such as unexpected combinations of data, can also result in unprocessed messages. Thus, the more workflow you use, the more need you will have for appropriate support when it goes wrong. This is all manageable, but the biggest problem with workflow lies in the very fact that many areas can benefit from its use. This can result in delays during implementations because of the additional design, building, and testing involved.

1.6 Summary

Invoice verification in SAP is a solid and efficient process. But try wherever possible to use the standard SAP functionality covered in this chapter. This will ensure that you gain maximum benefits for the least possible effort.

In Chapter 2, we will be looking at the functionality in more detail, and this should enable you to design an invoice verification process to suit your needs.

2 Specific Functions in Detail

This chapter will provide the information you need to design and use the main functions within SAP Invoice Verification. Detailed configuration information is described in Chapter 4, and that chapter will also show you how to set up the functionality in a way that best suits your business or your client.

2.1 The Goods Receipt-Based Invoice Verification (GR-Based IV) Flag

This one flag has been responsible for more problems in invoice verification than any other flag or setting available. So please fully understand its use before you apply it. It seems at first that this flag that should be set every time, given that you want your invoices to be matched against your goods receipts (GR), but this is not what this flag does.

This flag indicates that the invoice should be verified against an individual goods receipt rather than a purchase order (PO) line (in version ERP 6 this field title has changed slightly to GR-Bsd IV). Using this flag incorrectly can bring about overly complex business processes and can make the SAP Invoice Verification function appear weak. We would hazard a guess that if you are experiencing significant problems with your invoice verification functions you have probably used this flag extensively.

The main design problem is that the flag does not actually do what its name suggests.

Before you consider using this flag, you must realize that it is definitely *not* a flag that you set to ensure that the invoice is verified against goods receipts. Standard invoice verification in SAP already does this for POs that involve goods receipts. There is no flag to turn this on or off, as it involves basic three-way matching, and there would be no point in having an invoice verification function that does not check the goods receipt data when it is available. Figure 2.1 shows the **GR-based IV** flag on the item invoice tab of a purchase order (as viewed using transaction ME23N).

What Does the GR-Based IV Flag Do?
To understand the flag's function, you have to think of it as a *delivery-note-based* invoice verification flag rather than a *goods-receipt-based* invoice verification flag. If you switch it on, then you can verify your invoices against individual receipts posted for the purchase order line instead of a single line summary of receipts posted for the purchase order line. This is very useful if your vendor insists on sending you invoices that detail each delivery instead of a summarized invoice that just shows one line for each line on the purchase order.

There are many reasons, however, why you should try to get the vendor to submit summarized invoices. The main reason is that it will take longer if you have to match

Figure 2.1 GR-based IV Flag on Item Details of the Purchase Order

www.sap-press.com 19

individual receipts. Moreover, some invoices may be blocked for payment, not because we believe that the vendor should not be paid but simply because we cannot match the invoice lines against the appropriate receipts that we have posted. It is far better to pay the vendor if you know that you actually owe them the money, instead of risking vendor action by defaulting because you can't match the payment to an individual receipt.

Suppose you receive an invoice from a vendor for a total of € 1,000 for 100 pieces of an item. The invoice shows 20 different deliveries for varying quantities, with a delivery-note number alongside each. The total you have received is 100 pieces, and the purchase order price is € 10 each. The total quantity proposed by the system thus matches the total value of the invoice. For some reason, however, the individual delivered quantities do not match, perhaps because your goods-receiving department transposed a couple of delivery note numbers. With the GR-based IV flag set *on*, you have to investigate what happened, and this will take time. So you cannot pay the vendor, even though it is asking for a payment that matches exactly what it is entitled to.

In more than one implementation, this has caused vendors to refuse to take any more orders from the company because payments are constantly being made late, or not at all. If the flag had been set *off* instead, the invoice could have been matched quickly and accurately and paid on time.

The Risks of Setting the Flag Off

You should remember that by using three-way matching in invoice verification, the system will not pay a vendor an amount that is not actually owed to that vendor (based on the goods receipts that have occurred and the purchase order price). So, if the flag is set off, there is no greater risk of overpaying the vendor than there is with the flag set on. The only risk that increases is the risk of paying for the *wrong delivery*. Even if this occurs, you will not have overpaid, nor will you pay for the delivery twice (three-way matching will prevent this).

If the total value and quantity match, but the wrong delivery note has been paid for, there is no significant damage. When the other delivery arrives for the same value and quantity, this invoice will be paid and the end result will be the same. If the total value and quantity do not match, the invoice will not balance, and either will be investigated or blocked for payment. Again, no damage will be done.

It could be argued that by having the flag set *on* you will highlight errors earlier in the process because there is a more detailed matching during invoice verification. The problem with this argument is that you now will have a more complicated process on every invoice even if it is correct and matches fully, and the vendor will not be overpaid in any case. The low risk, the time saved on every invoice posted, and the likelihood that vendors will be paid on time are advantages to setting the flag *off*.

The Risks of Setting the Flag On

The main problem here is that you will not be able to post an invoice before you have posted the goods receipt, and you may wish to do so. There can be many benefits to posting an invoice even if the goods receipt has not yet been posted; we will cover these benefits later in this chapter.

Here is the basic concept behind using the flag: No goods receipt equals no invoice. In this way, you are adding complexity to the process for little or no benefit. If you receive an invoice before the goods receipt has been posted, and you have the flag set *on*, then you have two main options.

You can exit the transaction and file the paper invoice for re-keying at a later date when the goods receipt has been posted (although, it isn't clear how you will know when this has happened). Alternatively, you can *park* the invoice for later processing. Either way, you now will have to process the invoice at least twice and possibly more often if you think the goods receipt has been posted and it hasn't.

It is important to ensure that the invoice-parking function is not used as a regular step in the invoice verification process. It has a specific use, and that is to allow the user to exit the transaction before all of the data has been entered or verified, without losing the data entered so far. By using the GR-based IV flag, you will increase the need for parking and therefore increase the complexity of the process.

This parking function is designed to be used when you don't have time to finish the transaction; perhaps you have to deal with another call, or you have to go home and you don't want to lose the data you have keyed. It should not be used just because the goods receipt hasn't yet been posted. It is certainly not designed to be used as part of the total process of matching invoices. If you use it this way, you will find that it does not have all the functionality you need, and you will therefore experience various problems, such as missed invoices and duplicates. You may find that some parked invoices are overlooked and remain on file for some time. For example, someone who didn't know that there already was a parked invoice for this item may have posted the invoice again.

Setting the flag *on* may leave you with less than perfect alternative solutions, whereas if the flag was set *off* you could post the invoice even though the receipt had not yet been keyed. This has the advantage that you no longer have to process the invoice again once the goods receipt has been keyed. It would have been blocked automatically when it was posted because of the quantity variance that resulted because the receipt had not been keyed, and it will remain blocked for payment until the receipt occurs.

There is no automatic release of invoices as such, but if you run the Automatic Release function every night it will release those invoices with blocks that are no longer valid. You run the function using transaction MRBR as a batch job with the **Release automatically** flag set as seen in Figure 1.11. In this case, if the goods receipt is posted (for the correct quantity), the blocking reason is no longer valid, and the invoice will be released for payment (if no other blocks exist).

Thus, with the **GR-based IV** flag set *off*, an invoice without a goods receipt just needs to be posted once and does not need to be processed manually again when the stock arrives. This situation is much better than having to post the invoice, switch it to parked status, wait for the goods receipt, and then process the invoice again to post it.

In some countries, there is also a potential tax benefit from fully posting an invoice even though it does not match correctly (i.e., no receipt has yet been received). This benefit cannot be achieved if the invoice is parked rather than posted. Please check your local tax laws to verify if this is the case in your country.

On Vs. Off

In our opinion, the advantages of setting the flag *off* far outweigh the disadvantages. This does not mean that the flag serves no purpose, as there are situations where it is necessary. It is essential, for instance, if the vendor insists on matching invoices delivery by delivery. We emphasize "insists" because we would always try to persuade the vendor not to demand this if at all possible.

There are also certain settings in SAP that will force you to have the GR-based IV flag set on. External services POs involving service entry sheets and self-billing (known as ERS in SAP and covered in Section 2.4) need this flag to be set *on* so that the correct data is captured at goods-receipt stage. If you are using these functions, you have no choice but to set this flag *on*, but you will experience some of the issues mentioned above.

The chances are that the business users may prove difficult to convince that they do not need this flag to be set *on* for the majority of purchase orders.

We have had many a heated debate over this in several implementations, and it has taken many attempts to convince the users to even carry out a test. To avoid this, make sure that you point out very early in the project that the name of the flag is misleading. Point out that it should be thought of as the *Delivery-note-based* invoice verification and explain the negative effects.

Users will certainly want to carry out goods-receipt-based invoice verification (three-way matching) and so they will be convinced that they need this flag to be set *on* every time. The problem is that if the flag is used in this way, the complexity involved is wrongly assumed to be due to complexity in the way SAP Invoice Verification works.

If you set up invoice verification correctly and only use this flag when absolutely essential, then SAP Invoice Verification will be seen as an excellent process that is simple to operate and very efficient.

How the Flag Works

If the flag is set on a purchase order line item and a goods receipt is posted, then a delivery-note number (or bill-of-lading number if appropriate) must be entered at the time of posting. This normally is done using transaction MIGO.

2 Specific Functions in Detail

It makes sense to set these fields as mandatory, using the configuration options for MIGO, if you would normally expect all receipts to have some kind of reference-document number. Figure 2.2 shows the MIGO screen and the fields available for this purpose (**Delivery Note** and **Bill of lading**).

The material document now has a unique identifier for every goods receipt posted against this purchase order line item. This can be used within invoice verification to display a separate line on the display for every delivery note.

Entering an Invoice for a Purchase Order with the Flag Set On

This results in a slightly different display than you would see normally. You will now see a separate line for each delivery with the delivery-note or bill-of-lading number displayed to enable a full match against the invoice (a bill-of-lading is a type of shipping document detailing the contents of a consignment).

Figure 2.3 shows the invoice screen for a purchase order with only one line item that has had four separate receipts, each with a different delivery-note number. One line is displayed per delivery note instead of the one-line-per-purchase order line because the **GR-based IV** flag is set on the purchase order line item.

To post the invoice, you must match each delivery contained on the printed invoice from the vendor to a line on the invoice verification display. You cannot add lines or enter a quantity if the system proposes zero, which indicates that no goods receipt is awaiting an invoice. This is because when the flag is set *on* you cannot

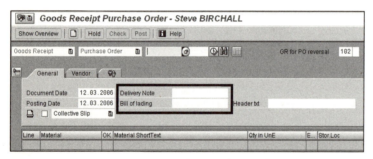

Figure 2.2 Relevant Fields of MIGO (Goods Receipt) Transaction

Figure 2.3 Invoice Posting with GR-Based IV Flag Set On (Multiple Receipts)

2.1 The Goods Receipt-Based Invoice Verification (GR-Based IV) Flag

Figure 2.4 Invoice-Posting with GR-Based IV Flag Set Off (Multiple Receipts)

post an invoice for something that has not yet been received. The quantity you enter against each delivery line displayed on the invoice screen can be less than or equal to the quantity received, but it cannot be more than the quantity received.

If the invoice is for more than the system is proposing, you either have to park the invoice and carry out a further receipt before the invoice can be posted or reject the invoice altogether and not post it.

Entering an Invoice for a Purchase Order with the Flag Set Off

This results in a normal display with one line per purchase order line. The quantity proposed on that line will be the quantity remaining to be invoiced. Figure 2.4 shows the invoice screen for a duplicate purchase order that has had the same number of receipts but where the **GR-based IV** flag is set *off*.

If the proposed line is zero or less than the invoice quantity, you simply change it to match the invoice quantity. As long as the invoice lines are mathematically equal to the total invoice value, you can post the invoice.

The system will either leave the invoice available for payment or block it if the tolerances have been exceeded.

You need not do anything with this invoice after this point. If the extra quantity arrives later, it will be checked again and released if appropriate. This is a much simpler and safer process.

Where is the Flag Set?

The flag is set on the purchase order line (**Invoice** tab) and can be defaulted from the purchasing Info Record if required. Figure 2.5 shows the flag on the Info Record (displayed using transaction ME13).

Figure 2.5 Flag on the Info Record

The flag can be changed during purchase order creation or amendment, if required. If a goods receipt has already been posted, then you cannot change the flag. This rarely presents problems, because the invoice can still be posted either way.

www.sap-press.com 23

2 Specific Functions in Detail

Figure 2.6 Purchase Order Example with Charges Detailed

2.2 Delivery Charges (Planned and Unplanned)

Delivery charges include freight, customs duty, and insurance. These charges may be known at the time that the purchase order is created, or they may be known at the time the invoice is posted.

It is far better to include these on the purchase order (as pricing conditions) wherever possible. Not only will the costs be posted against the material (as they should), but they will also be processed using the three-way invoice verification functionality and checked against the vendor's invoice.

Difference Between Planned and Unplanned Delivery Charges

The differences between planned and unplanned delivery charges are quite clear. Planned delivery charges are added to the material price as pricing conditions on the purchase order, whereas unplanned delivery costs are posted at the invoice verification stage. Planned charges are visible, controlled, auditable, financially appropriate, and thus are the correct method of posting such charges.

There are situations, however, where you simply will not know the charges when creating the purchase order. In these cases, you have no choice but to post the charges as unplanned at the invoice verification stage. It is important to understand the differences between planned and unplanned charges, and especially the financial postings that are involved (i.e., what accounts are used and what values are posted).

A Third Option

Another method often used is to post a separate line on the purchase order for these charges. The main problem with this approach is that there is no connection to the material being purchased unless you reference the material master record. If you do this, you must use an account-assignment category to ensure that the costs are posted to a separate account and that the receipt is not seen as a receipt of the material itself. This means that the actual costs are not reflected in the stock account of the material.

You may find this acceptable and decide to handle the posting of these costs later using allocations (these are ways of reallocating costs using financial postings). The standard approach with SAP, however, is to use the planned-charges method where possible and the unplanned option as an alternative.

As with almost anything in SAP, there are many ways of achieving the same result. This third option may be appropriate in your organization. It does have the advantage of providing full three-way matching at invoice time, and you may want to deliberately separate the costs from the actual material costs.

Using this option, you also can add delivery costs to the purchase order as a new line even after the materials have been received, achieving some flexibility. Make sure, though, that it provides the correct financial updates for your requirements. Figure 2.6 shows an example of a purchase order where the delivery charges are detailed on a separate order line.

2.2 Delivery Charges (Planned and Unplanned)

Planned Delivery Charges

To use planned delivery charges, you need to ensure that the correct condition types have been configured. The standard condition types are normally more than sufficient, and you will very rarely need to generate new ones. At most, you would normally just have to ensure that the correct accounts are linked to each condition type via automatic account determination (see Section 3.2).

There is one important setting on the condition type that you need to be aware of. This is a vendor setting that enables you to specify a different vendor for the delivery charges (as opposed to the main vendor on the purchase order) at goods-receipt stage (MIGO).

If you are not sure you will need to use this option, configure the condition type so that it is switched to *on* and available. That way, you can simply ignore the entry if you don't need to specify a different vendor at GR stage, and the system will use the default vendor; i.e., it will assume that the charges will be paid to the same vendor that was specified on the PO for these charges.

With this flag set *off*, you cannot specify or change the vendor at GR stage and this may well be exactly what you want to achieve. Changing the vendor at GR stage could be seen as a financial risk: Couldn't the person posting the GR "divert" the vendor's fees to another vendor? We would recommend that you only use this option if you are sure that you have mitigating controls that will reduce the opportunity for fraudulent use of this option. Figure 2.7 shows the configuration screen of a pricing condition type, with the flag highlighted.

When creating the purchase order, add the appropriate condition types (remember these can be at the header or line level of the PO) and assign the appropriate values

or percentages. If the charge is to be paid to a different vendor, then you should:

- Go to the conditions tab of the purchase order.
- Select the condition type by clicking on the select box to the left of the condition type.
- Click on the details icon (the magnifying glass).

Figure 2.8 shows the condition tab on the purchase order and the icons to select.

You will then see a vendor field, and you can enter the vendor that you will pay the charges to. Figure 2.9 shows the vendor field on the condition type.

Figure 2.7 Pricing Condition Configuration Screen Showing Vendor Option

Figure 2.8 Conditions Tab on Purchase Order

2 Specific Functions in Detail

If you are not sure which vendor will be used, you can leave this field blank, and it can be entered at goods-receipt stage providing that the flag has been set *on* for this in the configuration of the condition type.

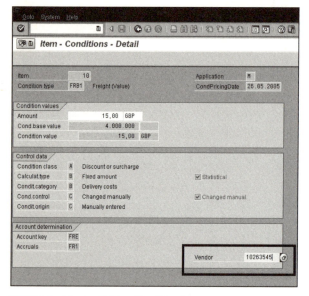

Figure 2.9 Vendor Field on Condition Type

You have two main options when dealing with additional charges like this. You either can enter the delivery condition types on the item line conditions of the purchase order, or you can enter them as header conditions by clicking on the conditions tab of the header. Figure 2.10 shows the **Header Conditions** tab on the purchase order.

The main difference is in how the costs are then apportioned. Header delivery costs are spread evenly across the items on the purchase order, while item delivery costs are only applied to that item. If the charges relate to an item, post them as item conditions. If the charges are per purchase order, post them as header conditions.

If the delivery condition types don't appear on the header or item-conditions tab, then you need your Materials Management (MM) consultant (who deals with purchasing configuration) to ensure that the condition types are included in the correct price calculation schema and treated correctly in the calculations.

There are several delivery-condition types to choose from, and you should choose the appropriate condition type for your purpose. Some involve a single charge that does not vary according to the quantity or value, and some are proportional.

These condition types can have pricing scales: One charge for up to x items and a different charge for more than x items and so on. They also can be set up so that they relate to volume or weight if appropriate. These condition types should be added to the purchase order before the goods receipt. They cannot be added afterwards.

When the goods receipt is posted (normally using Transaction MIGO), the system will assume that the delivery charges are now to be available for invoicing. If the condition type has been configured correctly, you will

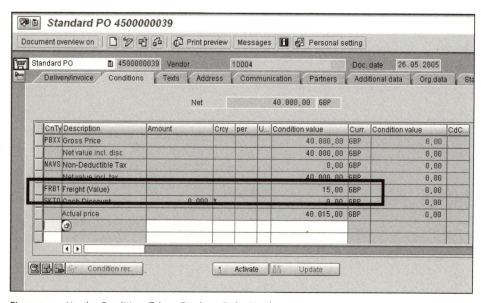

Figure 2.10 Header Conditions Tab on Purchase Order Header

also see an additional tab in MIGO that will allow you to enter or change the vendor responsible for the charges.

Posting Planned Delivery Charges in Invoice Verification

In invoice verification, you have to clearly indicate whether the invoice you are posting includes delivery costs. Your choices are as follows:

- The invoice has the material charges and delivery charges combined.
- The invoice has material charges only.
- The invoice has delivery charges only.

The options are selected from a pull-down list on the main screen of transaction MIRO. Figure 2.11 shows the pull-down list.

If the invoice contains both delivery charges and material charges and these are to be paid to the same vendor, then you can leave the vendor-number field in the details window of MIRO to default from the purchase order. Then use the drop-down list to select the appropriate option: **Goods/service items + planned delivery costs.**

However, if you are posting the delivery charges only, and if they are being paid to a vendor other than the one responsible for the items being purchased, you must enter in the vendor field on the MIRO screen the vendor being paid for the delivery charges. In this case select **planned delivery costs** from the pull-down list.

If the invoice is only for the item/service costs, do not enter the vendor number and select **goods/service items** from the pull-down list.

Enter the purchase order number, and the screen will then show the values that the system has calculated are due, based on the selection you made to indicate whether delivery charges or material charges (or both) are to be included.

The advantage of using planned delivery charges on the PO is that it introduces genuine three-way matching. The delivery charges will only be shown if the items or services have been received and the value will be the value entered on the purchase order (multiplied by the quantity received if the charge is relevant to quantity). As with a normal invoice, you can (and should) change the details proposed by the system to match those on the paper invoice. The system will then carry out the normal checks to see if the invoice balances and to determine if payment should be blocked.

For stock items, the delivery charges are posted to the stock account at the goods-receipt stage. This posting is subject to the rules regarding standard or moving average price controls, as discussed in Section 3.5. Any variances arising from a difference in invoice value will cause cor-

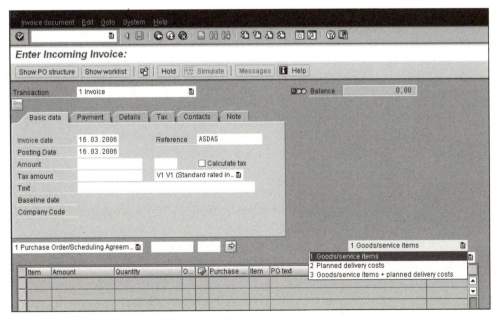

Figure 2.11 Pull-Down List on the MIRO Transaction

2 Specific Functions in Detail

rection postings to the stock account. Again, this is subject to the standard or moving average price controls.

For items posted directly to a consumption or expense account, the value of the delivery charges will be passed to that account.

The appropriate goods receipt/invoice receipt (GR/IR) clearing accounts will be updated and separate clearing accounts for the delivery charges and material charges can be used. See Section 4.3 to learn how to configure these.

We recommend that you use planned delivery charges wherever possible. If you are unable to enter the delivery charges or vendor until invoice verification, then unplanned delivery charges should be used.

Unplanned Delivery Charges

If no delivery charges have been stored on the purchase order and delivery charges are contained on the invoice (a process that may be agreed upon with the vendor), then you have to enter them manually at the invoice verification stage. If you need to enter delivery charges that are not included on the purchase order during invoice verification, you have two main options.

You can add an additional line in transaction MIRO and assign the charge to a specific general ledger account, providing the option of allowing lines to be added to the invoice to post direct to a G/L has been configured. Alternatively, you can enter the value in the unplanned delivery charges field, as shown in Figure 2.12.

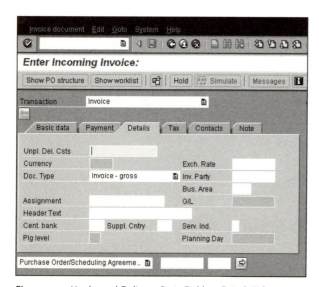

Figure 2.12 Unplanned Delivery Costs Field on Details Tab

The advantage of the second of these two methods is that associated functionality was designed for this purpose. On the other hand, merely adding an extra line to the invoice is perfectly acceptable if you believe that the financial postings will meet requirements.

By using the field provided instead of a separate line, you have the advantage of being able to automatically spread the charges equally across the invoice lines (by value). You need to realize, though, that the cost is not spread only across the lines on this current invoice; it will be spread across the total invoiced value to date for this purchase order.

There is also an option controlled by configuration (see Section 4.4), and this indicates how you want to handle the unplanned delivery charges entered in this field. You can either spread them across the invoice lines (which is the default), or you can have them posted to separate accounts automatically. This setting is controlled at the company-code level, so you should decide to use one method for all invoices relating to that company code.

One disadvantage of unplanned delivery charges is that they cannot be checked using three-way matching. As a result, values entered here will be passed along for payment as long as the rest of the invoice is fully matched within tolerances.

A Third Option

There is yet another option available if you must control invoices for additional charges by three-way matching. You can use a subsequent debit instead of using the unplanned delivery charges field.

To do this, you raise the subsequent debit (as detailed in Section 2.8) and enter the charge manually against the relevant item lines, splitting the costs in whatever proportion you want to. You can even post these against a different vendor if required, by changing the defaulted vendor in the details tab of the invoice-header screen.

Remember that subsequent debits are merely value-only invoices, so this additional invoice will not affect the quantity invoiced but only the value invoiced.

This method has the advantage of passing the costs directly to the material/consumption accounts. Moreover, the invoice will be blocked if this additional value exceeds the purchase order's value. We prefer this option to the use of the unplanned-delivery-costs field, and we suggest that you try this on your test system to see the full effect. You may find it the best option to handle your unplanned delivery charges, depending on your requirements.

SAP often gives you many options, and the problem is determining which one is most appropriate for your implementation.

2.3 Tolerances

There are many tolerances that relate to invoice verification available, and you don't have to configure them all. Some of them may not be relevant for your implementation. It is important to understand that you have to think of these tolerances as controlling whether an invoice should be blocked. They are not used to determine if an invoice can be posted (saved).

Why Have Tolerances?

What is the point of tolerances? While it is true that you would not want vendors to be overpaid, you should consider the true cost of investigating small differences.

Let's use an example. A vendor has invoiced you for a total of € 10,000 for a purchase order including 100 items at a price of € 99.90 for each item. This has resulted in a difference of € 10. If you calculate the true cost of passing this invoice to the buyer for investigation, and the buyer contacting the vendor, then changing the purchase order to reflect the correct price, and the invoice verification clerk then re-matching the invoice, it certainly will come to far more than € 10.

It is for your company to decide if this true cost is justified, and this decision may well be influenced by the general standard of vendors that you use. It may be acceptable that your vendors take advantage of this tolerance, or it may be that the sheer frequency of such small differences makes it unacceptable.

That is exactly what the tolerances are there for: They enable the implementation team to work with the financial department to decide what, if any, differences will be allowed.

What Kind of Tolerances are There?

It is also important to realize that the tolerances in invoice verification relate to more than prices or values. There are tolerances that relate to dates, and one such tolerance is linked to the delivery date. This is very useful when a vendor has sent an invoice too early, something often done deliberately.

The **delivery-date** tolerance can be used to check the invoice date against the requested delivery date. A vendor will sometimes send the goods and invoice early, and without this tolerance the invoice would normally be paid because the invoice quantity would match the goods-received quantity. This special tolerance however, would check the invoice date and delivery date and block the invoice for payment because of the early invoice.

Early invoices cost your company in the following ways:

- You lose cash-flow due to early payment.
- You have to pay to store the goods until the date you actually need them.

Special Tolerances

Certain special tolerances don't seem important at first but in fact are extremely useful. One example is the **Moving Average variance** tolerance. If you do not use moving-average prices (MAP) in your implementation, then this tolerance is not required. Section 3.5 gives more information on moving-average prices.

As explained earlier, when an invoice is posted with a variance in value, the financial postings still occur but the invoice is blocked for payment. This can cause major problems if you are using MAP, because the incorrect invoice price will affect the MAP even though the invoice did not match and was blocked.

For instance, suppose you have a material that has a MAP of € 100 per item, and you post an invoice with a per-item value of € 1,000 for this material, perhaps because of a keying error by the vendor or invoice verification clerk. In this case, the MAP will be increased significantly even though the invoice will be blocked for payment.

That is why SAP has provided this tolerance. You can set it (normally with a reasonably large tolerance) so that when an invoice is posted for an item a warning message is displayed indicating that posting this invoice will cause a significant change in the MAP.

This can prevent future problems if the item is consumed at the potentially artificial cost. Remember that if the invoice is subsequently corrected, this will not correct the values used in any postings that occurred between the initial invoice posting and the correction.

> **Note:** The same tolerance is used during goods-receiving to indicate significant changes to the MAP caused by a goods receipt at a value different from the current MAP, because of a different purchase order price.

Other Tolerances

Another useful tolerance is related to those invoices that contain lines that do not relate directly to a purchase order. These cannot be three-way matched, and so SAP provides a tolerance that can be set to block an invoice line that does not relate to a purchase order if it exceeds a certain value. Another user can then check this blocked invoice line to ensure that the invoice is valid.

One special tolerance that must be used correctly is the one called **Form small differences automatically**. It is vital that this is used only to allow extremely small differences, such as rounding errors; otherwise it will allow invoices to be paid even though they do not match.

It is quite normal for this tolerance to be set to a value as small as € 1, which is a typical variance caused by tax postings such as value-added transaction (VAT). This tolerance is also unique because it does not affect whether the invoice is blocked.

It influences the mathematical check carried out to ensure that all invoice lines and taxes add up to the total invoice value that has been entered. We have seen this tolerance set to very high values by mistake, and this has always resulted in many problems throughout the invoice process.

Configuring the Tolerances

Configuration of the tolerances is covered in Section 4.4 in detail, but there are some tips that can help get you started.

First, you must ensure that you have all of the required tolerances set up for your company code or codes. We find that the easiest way to do this is to copy the standard tolerances that SAP has configured for the company code 0001. This way, you will at least have the minimum set of tolerances, and all that you will have to do is to change the values of the tolerances to suit your requirements. Some transactions will expect certain tolerance keys to exist for the company code being used and will report errors if they do not exist. By using the 0001 tolerances, you can avoid this problem.

For the development client, we normally copy the following tolerance keys from company code 0001, unchanged, as shown in Figure 2.13. This will at least allow you to use the system before you configure the final tolerance settings.

Co...	Company Name	TlKy	Description
0001	SAP A.G.	AN	Amount for item without order reference
0001	SAP A.G.	AP	Amount for item with order reference
0001	SAP A.G.	BD	Form small differences automatically
0001	SAP A.G.	BR	Percentage OPUn variance (IR before GR)
0001	SAP A.G.	BW	Percentage OPUn variance (GR before IR)
0001	SAP A.G.	DQ	Exceed amount: quantity variance
0001	SAP A.G.	DW	Quantity variance when GR qty = zero
0001	SAP A.G.	KW	Var. from condition value
0001	SAP A.G.	PP	Price variance
0001	SAP A.G.	PS	Price variance: estimated price
0001	SAP A.G.	ST	Date variance (value x days)
0001	SAP A.G.	VP	Moving average price variance

Figure 2.13 Basic Set of Tolerances Used as Starting Point

Each tolerance key is described in Section 4.4.

Error Messages Resulting from Tolerances

To ensure that you have the correct error-message settings for each tolerance, you can set the message to an **E** or a **W**. Messages set to **E** are treated as errors and will not allow the process to continue. Messages set to **W** are treated as warnings and can be ignored to allow the process to continue.

You can also configure different error message settings for each user or group of users, so that one user gets an **E** message and another gets a **W** message.

Figures showing the settings and full details are contained in Section 4.2. As an example of how this can be used, you may wish to prevent certain tolerances from being allowed unless they have been authorized. To achieve this, you need to set the error message to an **E** for non-supervisory users but set the message to a **W** for a supervisor.

When users get the **E** message preventing the invoice from being processed, they must ask a supervisor to post the invoice. The supervisor will just get a warning message, but will be allowed to continue.

Note that some error messages are controlled from within the program or transaction. Even though you can change them in configuration, this will not always be used by the program and so the configuration is superseded by the program code

2.4 Evaluated Receipt Settlement (ERS)

ERS is basically self-billing. Here, the vendor will not submit an invoice and we will send the payment to the vendor based on what we have ordered and received. This is a very useful function that will save a lot of time and effort if used appropriately. It is designed to be used with vendors with whom you have good business relationships, and it works even better when used for inter- or intra-company purchases between different elements of your own business. The concept is very simple and follows standard business processes, even though it appears to be quite different from normal invoice verification.

How Does ERS Work?

If you use the standard three-way matching within invoice verification, the system compares the invoice value against the quantity received so far, multiplied by the price on the purchase order. If the vendor's invoice matches this, then it is passed for payment.

For the system to match the invoice, it must already know the values and quantities that are due to the vendor. If the system knows how much we owe the vendor, why wait for the vendor's invoice? Why not just send a payment at the agreed-upon time (according to the payment terms) for the values it has calculated? The benefit of this approach is that you would not need to use an invoice verification department at all, and there would (in theory) be no blocked invoices.

How Safe is the Process?

This process might appear to be slightly risky. What if you overpaid the vendor? They would certainly not be in a hurry to send the money back. While this is true, the fact remains that you can only overpay the vendor if your data is incorrect; e.g., having the wrong price on the PO or posting the wrong GR quantity. If this is the case, then you already have problems because this data is core data and should not be inaccurate.

Also this functionality is really designed for those vendors that you know and trust (within reason). Remember that you have full control over the purchase order price, and you actually carry out the goods receipt and indicate exactly what you have received, so the amount due to the vendor is known.

The possibility of overpaying is therefore low, and yet the benefits of removing the invoice processing step are high. Fewer people are required for the process, you are more likely to pay on time, and you are therefore in a stronger position to negotiate better prices. Some vendors will offer better deals just because you are prepared to use self-billing.

ERS for Inter- or Intra-Company Scenarios

If you are using purchase orders to buy and sell between different parts of your own organization, then ERS is recommended for the settlement of any related invoices. It seems strange when we see organizations buying from parts of their own business, generating invoices and matching them, and having such problems as blocked invoices due to minor mismatches. These organizations spend a lot of time and effort managing the matching process, especially when it comes to the GR/IR clearing account. If you really must invoice in this way (i.e., between different parts of your own organization), then consider ERS because it will prevent much wasted time and energy.

The ERS Process

The process is not complicated. You flag the vendor as being relevant for ERS. Figure 2.14 shows the flag on the purchasing-data view of the vendor master record.

This flag is then passed (via the Info Record if used) to the purchase order lines. The flag on the Info Record is set to the default, which is that ERS is applicable if the flag in the vendor data has been set. You only need to change this flag if you want this combination of material and vendor *not* to have ERS. If the flag is set on in the vendor master, then all purchases will be treated as ERS relevant unless you set the **No ERS** flag on the Info Record. Figure 2.15 shows the **No ERS** flag on the purchasing data of the Info Record.

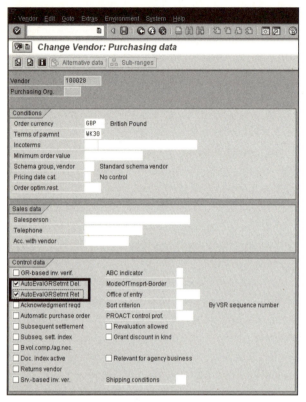

Figure 2.14 Evaluated-Receipt Flag on Vendor Master Record

Figure 2.15 The No-ERS Flag on the Info Record

When using this flag, the system will insist on a valid VAT code being specified in the purchase order (if VAT is relevant in the country involved). This is required because there is no invoice posting and so no opportunity to enter this later.

For an ERS-relevant PO line, the system creates an additional record at goods-receipt stage that is only used within the ERS processing. This record is used to speed up the process when the settlement program is used, instead of searching through all goods receipts for relevant records, it can just search through these receipts that are relevant for ERS. This is only needed by the settlement program and you should therefore not try to use this document for any other purpose or even try to display it, as it is purely an internal document.

The ERS Settlement Transaction

The ERS settlement transaction (MRRL) is run periodically. Normally this occurs monthly, but use whatever frequency is suitable for your requirements. This function actually mimics the invoice verification transaction MIRO. It creates an invoice document as MIRO does, but it uses the known quantities and values to complete the details of this document that would be manually entered in the MIRO transaction. The invoice will not be blocked for quantity or price reasons, because these are derived from the purchase order and goods receipt and so will match exactly, although other blocking factors could be applied, such as stochastic blocks (described in Section 4.7). ERS does not directly guarantee there will be zero blocked invoices, although it would reduce them to virtually zero, depending on your use of any of the special blocking options. Figure 2.16 shows the selection screen of MRRL.

The settlement program has an output type attached to it that will produce a printed (or faxed, emailed, etc.) document that details the transactions being settled. This output goes to the vendor so that it will know what the payment covers. The settlement does not directly trigger a payment. It merely creates the same type of invoice verification record that would normally be created by transaction MIRO. This record will be considered in the next appropriate payment run, taking into account the associated payment terms to ensure that it is not paid too early or too late. The posting date of the goods-receipt range should be entered, and these dates should be exact to ensure that there is no overlap or gap in the dates of each run (although double-paying for the same receipt will not occur).

Figure 2.16 Selection Screen of the ERS Settlement Transaction (MRRL)

2.5 Invoice Reduction

This functionality may be useful in certain implementations, but we don't see it as a widely used function. It fulfils a specific task and is only relevant when a mismatch occurs so that the vendor's invoice is larger than the amount due. Invoice reduction does not work when the vendor is asking for less than the expected amount. It is only used where you want the difference to be balanced out with an automatically generated credit note. This means that there are a limited number of scenarios where this is appropriate.

What Does Invoice Reduction Do?

It is easier to describe invoice reduction by using the following example.

A vendor has sent in an invoice for more than you were expecting and for a higher value than the value of the goods received against the relevant purchase order. You have contacted the vendor, and it has agreed that the invoice is wrong. In normal circumstances, you would have two options: Ask the vendor to send in a corrected invoice, or post the invoice and await a credit note.

With invoice reduction you have a third option: You can post the invoice and the credit note at the same time, in one transaction. The result is an invoice that matches, because the overcharge is offset by the credit note.

The invoice can be cleared, and the payment would be for the difference between the invoice value and the credit note value. This can save a lot of time and effort, but you would need the consent of the vendor to use this function. You will have to verify with your financial department whether posting an invoice in this manner is acceptable.

If you want to post the incorrect invoice without using invoice reduction, then the process would involve the posting of the incorrect invoice with the potential to corrupt the MAP if it is used. The invoice would be blocked for payment, and you would have to wait for a credit note to be received from the vendor.

Then you would have to post the credit note onto the system and finally run the MRBR transaction to clear the invoice for payment. The other option — not posting the invoice at all until the correct one has arrived from the vendor — means that you will have to cancel the invoice verification for this invoice and wait until the new one arrives, leaving open the possibility that a further mismatch might occur.

Many organizations opt to simply await a replacement invoice, because this does not present any significant problems. It is strange, though, that out of all of the SAP implementations that we have been involved in, not one of them has used the invoice-reduction process.

The Invoice-Reduction Process

For this process, you post the invoice in the normal way using transaction MIRO. When the difference is identified, you need to decide if you want to post it and block the payment or — if you are sure that it is a vendor error — post it using invoice reduction. If you wish to treat it as a vendor error, then choose the layout **Invoice Reduction** from the list of layout options on the **Enter Incoming Invoice** screen, as shown in Figure 2.17.

You will then be able to enter a **correction ID** in the appropriate field (scrolling to the right to see this field). The list will contain options that have been configured, and there would normally be one that indicates **vendor error**.

2   Specific Functions in Detail

Figure 2.17 Invoice-Reduction Selection from Pull-Down List

It is important that you not enter the corrected data from the vendor's invoice into the **Amount** and **Qty** fields as you would normally do. Just leave these as they are defaulted by the system. You must now enter the amount and quantity from the vendor's invoice in the specially provided fields for invoice reduction.

These fields are labelled **Invoice amount acc. to vendor**, and **Invoice qty acc. to vendor**. This is why you need to specify the invoice-reduction layout; otherwise these fields would not be displayed. Figure 2.18 shows the special fields on the invoice-reduction layout.

Figure 2.18 Special Invoice-Reduction Fields

Entering the data in these additional fields enables the system to calculate the variance value to use in the automatic credit that it will create. When you press **Enter**, you will see a window indicating the amount that will be reduced by the posting. As long as the value entered in these special fields (minus tax as usual) corresponds to the invoice value entered in the **Basic data** tab (taking tax into consideration), then the balance should be zero, and the invoice should post successfully.

The Financial Posting of the Difference
The difference will be posted to a special clearing account that is determined by automatic account determination using the transaction event key RKA. See Section 3.2 for details.

Ensure that the finance department has specified which general ledger account should be used, and request that the account be set up to accept automatic postings. The credit note that is automatically created also posts to the same clearing account, thereby balancing the posting.

> **Note:** Any credit posted via this function is not reflected in the stock account. The transaction is seen as a value correction relating to the payment of the vendor and not a variance of the cost of the materials received. Consequently, here is no impact on the MAP or price-variance account for the material.

The system sees the variance as an invoicing error. The end result is that the postings at goods-receipt stage were correct and so do not need to be adjusted. The payment to the vendor will also be for the price of the materials multiplied by the quantity received, and again no correction is necessary.

2.6 Pipeline and Consignment Stock Settlement

Invoice payments for pipeline materials and consignment stocks are treated in the same way. The basic concept that applies to both is that you only pay for the consumption of these items, and there is no purchase order to match against an invoice. Consignment purchase orders exist but are not valuated, and no invoices are matched against them; they are merely used to request a replenishment of the stock.

In effect, the vendors are paid via a form of ERS. The basic process is that the details of the consumption are collected from goods-movement records, and the value of the items (stored on special Info Records) is multiplied by the quantity involved in the movement. This calculation produces the amount due to the vendor. The settlement program is run periodically and creates an invoice verification record available for payment for the value concerned, as it does in ERS.

We have seen implementations where modifications have been made to allow invoices to be posted against consignment purchase orders, but this is not recommended, and many problems surface later because of the non-standard functionality.

The consignment purchase orders are meant to be unvalued and are only designed to be records that control the replenishment of stock. After all, the basic concept is that you pay for the items as you use them, and this practice is not normally linked to the quantity you ordered from the vendor.

If you want to link the purchase order to the invoice, then you must ask yourself if consignment stock is appropriate. Normal purchase orders may be more appropriate in this case.

Consignment Stock
Consignment stock is stock that you have available to use as and when you wish to. The stock remains the property of the vendor until it is used and does not appear in your accounts in any way. You pay the vendor for any stock that you have used since the last settlement. Purchase orders are used, but only to request the vendor to replenish the stock.

The goods receipts against these purchase orders do not cause any financial postings because the stock is still owned by the vendor. Financial postings only occur when the stock is consumed, written-off, scrapped, or transferred to your own stock.

These movements cause the value to be posted to the appropriate liability account awaiting settlement. The

2 Specific Functions in Detail

value is transferred from the liability account to the vendor account as an open item when the settlement occurs.

Something that appears strange at first is that any stock-count losses cause financial postings even though the stock does not belong to us. If we have lost some of the vendor's stock, we are liable to pay for it, and so we effectively have to treat it as being consumed. Therefore we owe the vendor for the stock we lost.

The consignment settlement transaction (MRKO) operates in a manner similar to the ERS transaction, and it is equally important to specify exact date ranges that do not overlap or have gaps.

You can use us the transaction either to display or settle the liabilities by using the appropriate flags. You must also indicate if you wish to settle consignment stock liabilities, pipeline liabilities or both by using the appropriate flags. Figure 2.19 shows the selection screen used for consignment stock settlement (and also for pipeline settlement) and the flags to indicate which is to be settled.

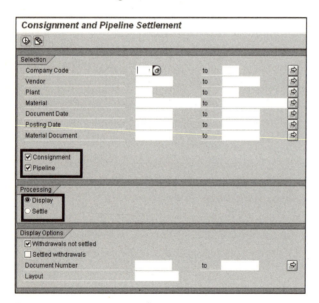

Figure 2.19 Consignment Settlement Transaction

Pipeline Stock

Pipeline materials are used for items you consume or sell but that you do not obtain via a purchase order and for which stock availability is assumed to be unlimited.

This category has been designed for utilities such as gas, electricity, or water, but is equally suited to anything that is available in unlimited quantity, that does not involve a purchase order, and that you pay for as you use

it. One of the biggest advantages is that this allows you to include these items on bills of materials (BOMs) and therefore collect consumption figures and post these costs to the material, if required.

Pipeline stock can be used for other situations. You are not limited to materials that are true pipeline materials. It could, for instance be used use to manage royalty and license payments. They do act in a very similar manner to pipeline materials, because these license fees and royalty payments are available in unlimited quantities.

We don't hold royalties and licenses in stock, we don't have to order them from the vendor, and they only have to be paid for as you use them. You can therefore include them in BOMs, etc., and capture the costs and consumption automatically, if required.

Pipeline liabilities are settled in the same way as consignment materials (in fact by the same program), and the only real difference between these and consignment materials is that they do not have stock levels or purchase orders. The value is stored on pipeline Info Records and these are used to calculate the liability to the vendor for each item consumed. Transaction MRKO is used, the same transaction used for consignment stock settlement.

2.7 Invoicing Plans

This functionality has been designed to be used for payments that are not directly linked to standard goods receipts or service confirmation. It enables you to use purchase orders for some situations such as recurring entries where you may have been tempted to use financial posting instead.

For instance, with no purchase order, the values involved would not show up in any reports on spending that obtain their information from purchase orders. Purchase orders also indicate future spending and commitments, and so this information would not be available either.

We would not be able to see that we have committed to spend x amount every month for N months with vendor Y for item Z. With a purchase order and an associated invoice plan we can do all of this while using the other related processes, such as authorization of the order and visibility of cash flow.

Invoicing plans are most likely to be used by the purchasing department for special purchases such as leases, rentals, or anything for which there are regular or staged payments.

There are two main types of invoicing plans, which are:
- Periodic invoicing plans, suitable for regular payments of the same amount
- Partial invoicing plans, suitable for partial payments of varying percentages, amounts spread over time, or milestones

In both cases, it is possible to post invoices because each payment is to be made (automatically or manually) without involving a purchase order for each payment.

Although these are both types of invoicing plans, they are treated differently, and it is best to deal with each separately.

Periodic Invoicing Plans

Periodic invoicing plans are designed for fixed-value payments that are paid at regular intervals, such as monthly, weekly, annually, or on set dates throughout the year. They are ideal for payments such as rentals, leases, or insurance.

Many organizations use the regular payments options available in the Financial module of SAP instead of invoicing plans, but these do not contain all of the information from a procurement point of view. Therefore, because a purchase order is involved, we have a value for each payment for each item and details of exactly when each payment should be made, rather than just having one value for each item. These POs show up in the relevant enquiries and reports within the standard MM functions.

This PO with an invoice plan would then allow matching against regular invoices without the need to post goods receipts, providing the vendor sends invoices for these payments. Better still, it can be used to trigger regular payments without waiting for an invoice using transaction MRIS, which involves an ERS-type process, also known as self-billing This means that once the PO has been set up correctly, payments would be automatically sent to the vendor as and when they fall due, without the need to carry out any action such as MIRO. Many vendors would not invoice for regular payments in any case.

Figure 2.20 shows the selection screen of the MRIS transaction. Note the **Test run** flag, which allows you to see the actions without updating anything.

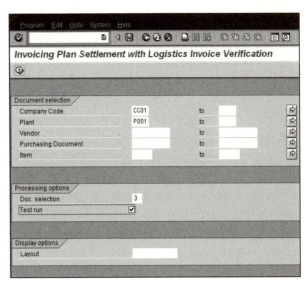

Figure 2.20 Selection Screen of Invoicing Plan Settlement Transaction (MRIS)

Partial Invoicing Plans

Partial invoicing plans are designed to be used when the payments to be made to the vendor are not regular amounts and when they are paid at irregular times, perhaps depending on specific events, milestones, or stages. The clearest example of this would be a situation where a vendor will be paid according to progress on a project or development that they have been tasked to do for us.

A building contract may have staged payments such as a percentage at commencement of the work, a further percentage when stage one is reached, further payments at each of the following stages, and perhaps a final payment several months after completion.

Payments such as these are normally only managed within the finance department because they are irregular and infrequent, and issuing separate purchase orders for each payment would be seen as not adding significant value. Using a partial payment plan could make the use of a purchase order feasible and add the associated benefits of visibility of the commitment and spending. The PO would contain the stages at which payment is due and the exact amounts or percentages to be paid at each stage.

2 Specific Functions in Detail

Figure 2.21 Receipt flags on Delivery Tab of Purchase Order

How Does the Process Work?

The purchase order is issued as normal, but you must select a non-valuated receipt or de-select the goods-receipt flag altogether on the **Delivery** tab of the purchase order item. Figure 2.21 shows the flags on the **Delivery** tab.

Invoicing plans cannot be used where a valuated receipt occurs, because this would then be used as the trigger for payment instead of the invoicing plan. The idea of the invoicing plan is to remove the need for goods receipts to be posted.

When you have entered the purchase order details, click on the **Invoice** tab on the item details section and then select **Invoicing plan**.

Figure 2.22 shows the **Invoicing plan** icon, which offers the option of choosing the appropriate invoicing-plan type.

Figure 2.22 Invoicing Plan Icon on Invoice Tab of the Purchase Order

The number and type of options presented will depend on what has been configured, but you could expect to see at least two options: partial and periodic.

When you have selected the appropriate type, you will be presented with a new window in which you can enter the details of the invoice plan. Some dates can be defaulted automatically if you have configured this option correctly. Figure 2.23 shows the new window that allows you to enter full details of the invoicing dates.

Figure 2.23 Invoice Plan Details Screen

A partial invoicing plan will allow you to enter dates and percentages that relate to the various stages of payments. You can leave the data blank if the details are not yet known, and you should then enter the stage details when they are known, before the payments are to be made.

You can either enter a percentage of the value for each stage or the actual value. The total percentage must add up to 100% and the total value must equal the value of the item line that is the subject of the invoicing plan.

A periodic invoicing plan will allow you to enter the payment schedule using regular or irregular dates. For the periodic invoicing plan, it is important to remember that the net price you entered against the item line on the PO screen is actually the individual payment amount, not the total to be paid over the term of the plan. So if the payment is € 100 every month for 10 months, the net price on the item line must be € 100, not € 1,000.

2.8 Subsequent Debits and Credits

Invoice Verification Relating to Invoicing Plans

You can simply post invoices against the purchase order in the same way as any other purchase order and the system will use the dates and stages on the invoicing plan to determine if the invoice should be blocked for payment. It is often better, though, to use the self-billing function specifically designed for invoicing plans (transaction MRIS), particularly for periodic invoice plans.

If you use transaction MIRO to post the invoice, then the system will match the invoice against any goods receipts that have been posted, providing the non-valuated GR flag was set on the PO line. They also can be matched against the dates of the stages or periods if no GR flag was set.

If you want to use self-billing, you can use the MRIS transaction (Invoicing Plan Settlement with Logistics Invoice Verification). Simply enter the selection criteria and execute the transaction, ideally in test mode initially. See Figure 2.21 for the selection screen of MRIS.

Basic Configuration for Invoicing Plans

You need to ensure that your materials-management team has configured the different types of invoicing plans that you need to be available for use. They will also need to configure any automatic date calculations such as start dates and periods.

There is no specific configuration in logistics invoice verification. The invoices are managed the same way as normal PO-related invoices.

2.8 Subsequent Debits and Credits

"Value Only"

The biggest problem with this functionality is the terminology used. The word *subsequent* does not explain exactly what is involved. If you substitute the words *value only* for *subsequent*, it helps clarify the true meaning. You are, in fact, posting a value-only credit or debit when you are posting a subsequent debit or credit.

Subsequent debits and credits are used to correct or amend invoiced values without affecting the invoiced quantities already posted.

Suppose vendor A sends in an invoice for 10 items at € 15 each and later realizes that the price was wrong and you should have been charged € 14 each. You cannot post a normal credit note, because this would involve a return of the items involved and in this case the quantity is to remain unaffected. It is only the value that needs to be corrected.

You therefore have to post a credit note that will only affect the value; i.e., a subsequent (or value-only) credit. A subsequent debit is the same process, but in this case the vendor is charging an increased value for the items, hence the word "debit."

Posting a Subsequent Credit

The normal invoice verification transaction (MIRO) is used to post a subsequent credit.

Select **subsequent credit** from the pull-down list in the transaction field. This will ensure that the quantity involved in the credit posting will remain unaffected. Figure 2.24 shows the pull-down list that allows you to specify a subsequent credit posting instead of an invoice.

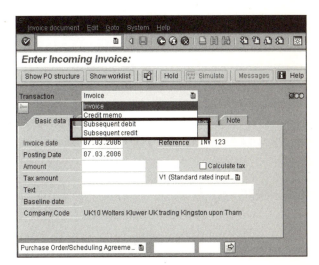

Figure 2.24 MIRO Pull-Down List Showing Subsequent Credit and Debit Options

Then follow these steps:

1. Enter the invoice details as you would normally, entering the total value of the credit (including taxes), and specify the tax value (or select the **Calculate tax** flag).
2. Enter the total value of the credit that applies to each line (not the value per item). For instance, if there is a one line invoice and the credit value is € 100, enter 100 in the **Amount** field on the invoice line. If the total credit was € 100, and this was to be spread equally over two lines, enter € 50 on each invoice line.

3. Enter a quantity, even though no items are being returned and this is a value-only credit. This quantity will be used to calculate how the value will be spread. A subsequent credit of € 100 for 100 items results in a price difference of € 1 an item. You must enter the quantity that the credit relates to. The credit may only refer to part of the quantity invoiced so far and therefore the quantity must be specified to enable the full calculation of the correction.

For example, the vendor has agreed that two of the items sent were substandard and has agreed to give you a credit of € 200 to compensate you. The order and invoice was for 100 items, and so you would enter the value of 200 and the quantity of two (replacing the quantity of 100 that would be defaulted by the system). This way, the postings will reflect that two of the items now cost € 100 less each.

This price variance will be posted to the stock or consumption account if the material uses MAP and if there are at least two items still in stock. It may also be posted to a price-variance account. These postings are explained in more detail in Section 3.5.

The total quantity invoiced remains unaffected because this is a value-only credit, but the purchase order history will be updated to reflect the subsequent credit and the values will be reflected in detail.

Posting a Subsequent Debit
To post a subsequent debit, follow the same process as when posting a subsequent credit, except this time you are posting a value-only invoice. Figure 2.24 shows the pull-down list where this option can be selected. This function is used when a vendor indicated that the price on an invoice was too low and the vendor had to send you an additional (or subsequent) debit.

The process also be used to post additional charges such as delivery charges, especially if you do not wish to use planned or unplanned delivery charges (as detailed in Section 2.3).

The basic concept is that you are being invoiced for additional values but the total quantity that has been invoiced remains unaffected.

As with subsequent credits, you still have to specify the quantity that is affected by the debit so that the exact effect of the debit can be correctly reflected against the items.

The purchase order history will reflect the extra debit in full detail.

Posting a Normal Credit
This kind of credit will affect the quantity invoiced as well as the value. It should only be used if the relevant items are either returned to the vendor or are to be treated as if you have never received them.

The process is the same as posting an invoice, only this time the values are reversed. That is essentially the only difference between a credit note and an invoice. The process, the checks, and even the screens are the same, but the signs are reversed (negative to positive and vice versa). Select the credit-memo option from the pull-down list in MIRO, and then do the following:

1. Enter the details as you would for an invoice.
2. When you have entered the details and specified the purchase order number, the system will suggest the quantity and value of the items that have already been invoiced.
3. Then change these to reflect the quantities and values that you are receiving credit for, or even enter them if the fields are blank.

The end result is a posting of the credit to the vendor's account, the credit record functioning as an audit trail, and an entry on the purchase order history to show the details of the credit.

2.9 Purchase Order Texts

There is a little-used function that can be very useful. It relates to the text that has been added to the PO header. It is not as complicated to set up and configure as it appears. It essentially enables texts from the purchase order header to be highlighted to the user entering the invoice for this PO during invoice verification. Ways to configure certain texts to be displayed are covered in Chapter 4.

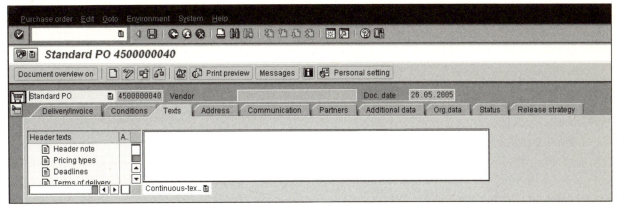

Figure 2.25 Purchase Order Header Texts

The Basic Process

The person creating a purchase order can enter texts in many places on the order, and each of the different kinds of texts can be used for different purposes. For example, the **Item** text on the purchase order can be printed along with the full order details when the document is printed, faxed, or emailed to the vendor. This text can give the vendor more information relating to the item being ordered. There are other texts at item level, and these can be used to store and display internal notes and memos that are not seen by the vendor but can be viewed by internal staff.

There are also header texts, which are used in the same way as item texts but with information relating to the whole purchase order and not to individual items. The person creating a purchase order can store at the header-level text that can be printed on the order or can be used as an internal memo. Texts such as these are often underused, but they can be very helpful in invoice verification. Figure 2.25 shows the header texts on a typical purchase order.

If configured correctly, selected texts can be displayed at the invoice verification stage. When the purchase order reference has been keyed into the MIRO transaction, the system checks to see if there are any texts on that purchase order that are flagged as relevant to invoice verification. If there are any, the system will use a pop-up window to inform the user that relevant texts exist. The user can then ask to view the texts from within that window. The text will be displayed, and when the user exits the texts will be returned to the invoice verification function to continue.

Within configuration, you indicate via flags if you wish to use this function, and then you must indicate which texts should be displayed. See Chapter 4 for the details of configuring this function.

If text is keyed into a PO header text that has not been flagged as relevant to invoice verification, then no window will be displayed at the invoice stage. The window only appears if text has been entered in a text that has been flagged.

An Example of How to Use this Function

To use this function, you need to do the following:

▶ Decide if you wish this option to be used in your organization. If so, then switch it on in configuration (See Chapter 4).

▶ Decide which purchase order header text or texts should be highlighted to the user when an invoice is being posted.

We recommend you get your materials-management consultant to configure an extra text element on the purchase order header, specifically designed to hold invoice-relevant notes. However, you can simply choose to use existing text elements if you wish. The advantage to creating a new element is that it can be named "invoice verification text," so it will be obvious to the user that this will be seen by the invoice department when an invoice is keyed.

It is not always obvious why you need to highlight a message to the invoice verification clerk, so let us consider the situation. Invoice verification works on the principle of three-way matching. If the vendor sends in an invoice that matches the quantity delivered at the price on the purchase order, then that vendor will be paid at the appropriate time, automatically.

There are occasions where you may not want the vendor to be paid automatically, even though the three-way match process indicates that all is well.

What if the purchase order is for multiple items, and you only want to pay for these when all of them have been received, because they are no use to you until you have every item from the vendor? If the vendor was to just send part of this order and then invoice for the same part of the order, the invoice would normally match and be paid even though you are left without those items that you need in order to use the items you already have received.

There may also be some important tax information that needs to be considered during the invoice posting, such as special withholding taxes. The person entering the PO may be the only person who knows this detail and so they can enter it in one of the flagged header texts, knowing that the text will be displayed during invoice verification.

This is where the notifiable texts can be particularly useful.

When the purchase order is raised, the header text "invoice verification text" (or whatever text has been flagged) is entered, stating something like: "This purchase order should only be paid when all items have been received; accept no partial invoices from the vendor."

Then, when the invoice is entered, the user will see a pop-up window announcing that there are relevant texts that should be read before continuing.

When the text is viewed, the user can then check to see if this is a full invoice by examining the purchase order items proposed by the system and act accordingly.

This text notification can provide functionality that at first appears to be lacking. It is well worth discussing with the main financial users to determine how relevant it is to their requirements. This functionality is often not implemented because it has not been requested, and it is often not requested because the user (and sometimes even the consultant) does not know that it is available.

2.10 New Functionality in Release ERP 6.0

The following sections focus on the changes and new functionality introduced in the latest release of SAP.

ERS for Delivery Charges

ERS only creates a payment request (invoice) for the items and or services on the PO. It will not manage any planned delivery costs that have been specified on the PO by using condition types. Such charges (freight, customs, insurance, etc.) are often not covered by a separate invoice; they are often paid to the vendor without this. Prior to release ERP 6.0 (also known as ECC 6.0 and ERP 2005) these charges would have to be settled via the posting of an invoice (sometimes a dummy invoice) in transaction MIRO. But now SAP has provided new functionality to enable you to pay delivery charges via the ERS approach.

There is a new report — RMMR1MDC — that is used to settle the charges. This report can be run via the new transaction MRDC.

The functionality works similarly to the "normal" ERS in that it depends on the GR taking place. The MRDC transaction can then be run at regular intervals to trigger the payment of these charges to the vendor.

The report will then generate one invoice (i.e., payment request) per condition type for the total quantity delivered.

There must be an entry in a configuration setting for each vendor that you want to activate for this functionality. The configuration setting is covered in Chapter 4. Only those vendors flagged as active in this configuration setting will trigger automatic payments of the delivery charges.

Note that the PO item for the goods or services need not be flagged as ERS-relevant. This function works for all POs that have planned delivery charges for the vendors flagged in configuration.

On the initial screen of transaction MRDC, shown in Figure 2.26, you can specify the selection criteria required. There is also a "test" flag to enable test runs before the actual run is performed (in our version of ERP 6.0, the field for the test flag has no title).

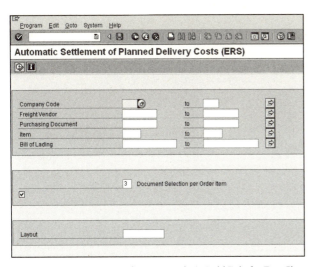

Figure 2.26 Inital Screen of MRDC, Lacking Field Title for Test-Flag Selection Box

Use the **Document Selection per Order Item** field to specify if you want an invoice per vendor, per PO, per PO item, or per bill-of-lading.

Execute the report in test mode first to verify exactly what will be settled and then run it without the test flag when you are sure that the result is as required.

There is also an additional flag on the ERS settlement function MRRL. This flag allows you to settle the payment for the delivery charges at the same time as the items or service (instead of running MRRL followed by MRDC).

Prepayment of Invoices

Not every vendor will accept credit terms (i.e., allow you time to pay after delivery); some will require payment in advance. Prior to ERP 6.0 this was normally handled by FI postings, or using the "down payment" functions. However down payments are meant to only be used where the vendor has asked for a *proportion* of the payment in advance, not where the full payment is required.

SAP now provides functionality specifically designed to handle the situations where the full amount due to the vendor is paid in advance, before the GR (if any) has been posted.

There are some configuration settings that have to be made to enable this functionality to be used and they are covered in detail in Chapter 4.

Once the configuration settings have been made, you can flag the vendor master record as being relevant for prepayment. This flag appears on the vendor "Payment transactions accounting" screen (company code level). The payment transactions accounting screen with its new field is shown in Figure 2.27.

The options are:

- Prepayment not allowed for this vendor
- Prepayment requested (i.e., prepayment assumed each time)
- Prepayment not before goods receipt has been posted
- Prepayment possible (i.e., prepayment can be posted but not defaulted as required)

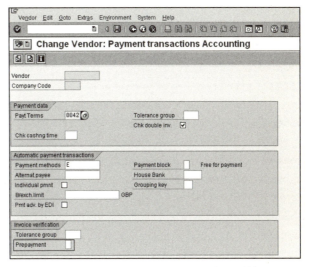

Figure 2.27 Payment Transactions Accounting Screen When Prepayment Options are Configured

These settings are held on the company code level and so can vary for each company code that deals with this vendor.

Select the flag that applies and this will trigger a new flag on the invoice-parking (MIR7) screen shown in Figure 2.28 to allow you to set or unset the flag at invoice parking stage.

To post a prepayment you must park the invoice. You do not use MIRO.

Once you have parked the invoice, this will trigger a payment to the vendor of the full amount specified on that invoice. The balancing entry will be a posting to a prepayment clearing account and this account will be cleared when the actual invoice has been posted.

The PO history will be updated to indicate that a prepayment has been made. This will appear as a parked invoice; on the header of the parked invoice you will see

2 Specific Functions in Detail

Figure 2.28 The Invoice-Parking Transaction Screen (MIR7) Showing New Prepayment Field

the flag indicating the prepayment. This is the same field as shown in the park invoice screen shown in Figure 2.28.

Also, if you check the financial document attached to this parked invoice you will see the prepayment posting details here.

The prepayment will be triggered in the normal payment run.

Note that this new function will not work on any PO that has the GR-Based IV flag set *on*, because this flag indicates that you want to post invoices against receipt documents and so the prepayment cannot take place. This also means therefore that the new function does not work with service POs (POs with Item category D) due to the fact that these have to have the GR- Based IV flag set *on*.

Variance Types

A new field has been added to the invoice verification screens (MIRO, MIR6 and MIR7). This field is known as **Variance Type** and is shown in Figure 2.29. This field is designed to be able to highlight the varying reasons for a mismatch. For example, one variance type can be used for the situation where the GR quantity varies from the invoice quantity. You can assign difference types of variance to different codes and this is designed to help you find these variances in invoices with multiple lines.

To take full advantage of this new field, you will need to use an appropriate Business Add-In (BAdI) to set the code in this field automatically, based on your own criteria. The BAdI is MRM_VARIANCE_TYPE. Your ABAP programmer can use this to ensure that the variance types are set as you require.

You will need to ensure that the line layouts that you use include this new field in an appropriate position. It will first appear towards the end of the line layout until you have moved it to a more appropriate position.

The invoice verification clerk can then sort the invoice lines into variance-type sequence and see the problem lines at the top of the line item display list instead of having to search through the document line by line looking to see if there is a problem. This function is particularly useful if you deal with a lot of invoices that have many lines to be verified.

Assignment Test

The assignment test is linked to the background processing of invoice verification (MIRA). The new functionality checks if an open goods receipt exists for the invoices entered in the list. The system will not attempt to process the invoice if no such GR has yet taken place. This should save time when processing long lists of invoices by skip-

2.10 New Functionality in Release ERP 6.0

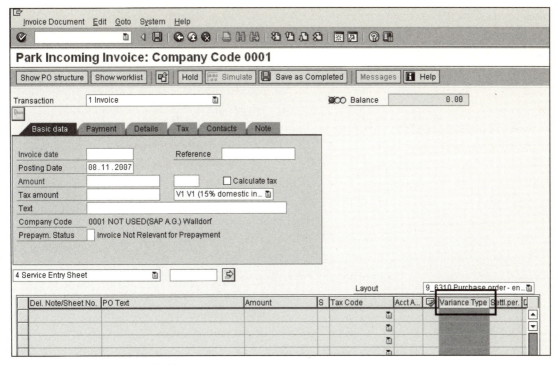

Figure 2.29 New Variance Type Field

ping those that cannot yet match because no receipts have yet been posted.

You need to make use of the BAdI provided for this function if you want to tailor the functionality in any way. The BAdI is WRF_MRM_ASSIGN_TEST and it provides two methods that you can use. You have DATES_REDE-TERMINE to change the dates of the first and last assignment tests, and you also have INVOICE_SAVE allowing you to change the status and various other fields when the invoice is saved.

Other New Functions and Options now Available

There are a number of additional new functions and options available as part of ERP 6.0; following are some of the major ones which impact those users with daily system interaction.

Invoice Document number display when posting

When you post an incoming invoice, the system can display the invoice document numbers generated in Materials Management, the document number of the accounting document in ERP Financials. and the number of the invoice reduction document where applicable.

These can be displayed in the status line for the following transactions:

- Enter invoice (MIRO)
- Park invoice (MIR7)
- Cancel invoice (MR8M)
- Invoice overview (MIR6)

They can also be displayed in the output list for the following transactions:

- Evaluated receipt settlement (MRRL)
- Revaluation (MRNB)
- Invoicing plan (MRIS)
- Invoice verification in the background (RMBABG00)

The setting to indicate whether the FI document number is also displayed is made at the user level via the parameter IVFIDISPLAY.

Segment Texts

In the transactions enter invoice (MIRO), park invoice (MIR7), and enter invoice for verification in the background (MIRA), you can use segment texts in the vendor line (field SGTXT) in the header on the basic data tab page. The entries in the document header text (BKTXT) field on the detail tab page are no longer copied into the segment text of the vendor line. Instead they are only copied into the document header text of the FI document.

Bundle Indicator
In the transactions, enter invoice (MIRO) and park invoice (MIR7), you can use the bundle indicator (field LOTKZ) in the header on the basic data tab page for the area public sector.

Archive Link
In the archive link: administration of stored documents transaction (OAAD), you can search help for invoice document numbers for business object 2081, document type MMILOGINV.

Multiple Account Assignments
On the screen for multiple account assignment in Logistics Invoice Verification, you can enter varying amounts and quantities. Manual calculation of amounts is no longer necessary, helping you to prevent invoices containing transmission errors.

Changing the Total Amount and the Total Quantity
The Total Amount and Total Quantity fields are now ready for input. If you enter a total amount or a total quantity, and choose Check (enter) or Back (transfer), this triggers automatic distribution to the relevant account assignment objects according to the distribution schema.

Changing Amounts and Quantities in Account Assignment Lines
If you change amounts and quantities in the account assignment lines, once you choose Check (Enter), the system adds the total amounts and total quantities. Any total amounts and quantities that have been recently entered are overwritten by the calculated amounts and quantities. The system issues a customizable error message. The automatically-calculated values are then used as default values. You can continue to change these values until you save the invoice. If rounding occurs, it is added to the items with the largest quantity or the greatest amount.

Enhanced Selection Criteria
The Document Type, Reference and Document Header Text selection criteria have been enhanced in the invoice overview transaction (MIR6):

You can select posted invoice documents, and display those invoices in the invoice overview according to the following scenarios:
- Created using BAPI_INCOMINGINVOICE_CREATE
- Created using evaluated receipt settlement (ERS)
- Created with logistics invoice verification using invoicing plan settlement
- Cancel another document
- Park

You can also select and edit held and parked invoices that have the status Held, Parked or Parked as Complete

The following additional information is displayed in the list of invoice documents:
- Origin of the invoice document
- Document type
- Document date
- Posting date
- Document header text

Processing Invoices via EDI
You can use a customer enhancement to assist in posting to Material or General Ledger accounts during processing of invoices incoming via EDI using Logistics Invoice Verification. To do this, use the enhancement MRMH0002 with the customer exit: EXIT_SAPLMRMH_015.

Transport Service Provider (in MIRA)
When you enter an incoming invoice for verification in the background (MIRA), you can assign a transportation service provider. If you select this, you can settle freight costs with transportation service providers in Logistics Invoice Verification.

New Report for Listing Invoice Documents
Logistics Invoice Verification offers you a new report display list of invoice documents (RMMR1MDI), which you can use to display a list of invoice documents. As an addition to the existing program invoice overview (transaction code MIR6), you have extended selection criteria and display options. For example, on the initial screen you can

make selections with criteria such as one-time customers, invoice gross amount, and entry date. You can also show an expert mode, which enables you to select at plant level by financial accounting document, General Ledger account posting, and Material posting. In the output list, the report shows both posted and held invoices. It does not show invoices without a corresponding FI document; such as invoices planned for verification in the background, or which the system has already verified as containing errors.

2.11 Summary

This chapter introduced the main elements of invoice verification. When used to their full capabilities, these options should provide you with an efficient and beneficial process.

Chapter 3 will focus on the financial elements, and Chapter 4 will show you how to configure the various functions mentioned in this chapter.

3 Financial Aspects of Invoice Verification

This chapter covers the financial elements of SAP Invoice Verification. As discussed earlier, the invoice verification function is normally designed and configured by the materials-management team in close coordination with the finance team. Therefore, this chapter deliberately avoids detailed financial terminology and describes the processes in basic terms.

3.1 Overview

The invoice verification function is designed to capture the details from the vendor's invoice and match them against expected quantities and values. The financial postings of a matched invoice are essentially the same as those of an unmatched invoice.

The only difference is that a blocking flag is set on the unmatched invoice. This will prevent payment to the vendor until the invoice has been fully matched or manually cleared for payment.

Postings involve the following:
- Vendor account
- Tax accounts where appropriate
- Price-variance accounts
- Goods-receipt/invoice-receipt (GR/IR) clearing accounts
- Stock accounts (mainly for price corrections caused by the invoice)

Other accounts, such as withholding tax, freight, customs, or duty may be involved depending on the circumstances. The accounts that will be posted to are determined automatically by the system, according to basic accounting rules and procedures.

3.2 Automatic Account Determination

This complex configuration step must be set up correctly in order to channel the various postings involved to the correct general ledger accounts.

This function is used in two ways, although it is essentially the same configuration step. These are:
- Setting up the automatic account determination for materials management. This is used for the majority of the materials management postings such as receipts, issues, or write-offs.
- Setting up the postings made during invoice verification. This is the same transaction, but a flag switches it between normal materials management postings and those postings involved in invoice verification.

It is important to realize what is being configured. You are merely entering the identifying number of the general ledger account that should be used in various standard account postings. You are not affecting the way that invoice verification accounts for the postings involved; this is built into the system and should not be altered. You are merely attaching the number of the account that you want posted to in each of the scenarios that will apply to your organization.

The process is covered in more detail in Section 4.3. This configuration must be carried out by the materials-management team and the finance team working together but not by one or the other alone. The materials-management team should be describing the various scenarios in invoice verification, and the finance team should be determining the correct general ledger account to be used for each posting relevant to each scenario.

3.3 The Goods-Received/Invoice-Received Clearing Account

This special clearing account essentially gives details of the balance of non-invoiced receipts or invoices received for items not yet received.

The total value in the account indicates the amount you need to have available in order to pay for the items you have received but have not yet paid for. This could be a negative amount if you have posted invoices before the goods receipts have been posted.

The clearing account appears to be based on values but is related more to quantities than to values, and this affects the way that it values any postings made. It has to clear the full value when the quantity invoiced matches the quantity received, regardless of the values involved.

For example, an invoice for 10 items at a value of €100 will clear a goods receipt of 10 items of any value (the same, higher, or lower) as long as the receipt relates to the same items on the same purchase order.

If there are entries in the account that have not cleared automatically, this indicates either that you have received invoices for items you have not yet received or have received items that have not yet been invoiced. It does not indicate a value-only discrepancy.

A GR/IR clearing account with many unresolved entries (and therefore a high value) normally indicates that the processes designed for invoice verification are less than ideal. This often happens when the **GR-based IV flag** has been used inappropriately (see Section 2.1). It also indicates that your vendors are probably being asked to wait for their money longer than is necessary (with all of the problems that this can lead to). If you do have a large value in this clearing account, first check whether the PO-to-invoice-posting process has been made more complex than it needs to be. Be sure to examine your use of the **GR-based IV** flag as mentioned throughout this book.

The clearing account is also a good source of data for various reports. On many occasions I have been asked if there is a standard SAP report that will show the purchase orders that have not yet been invoiced. The clearing account and the related reports and transactions will give full details of the balance of invoices yet to be received where a goods receipt already has taken place.

Sample Scenarios for the Use of the GR/IR Clearing Account

The use of the clearing account can be more easily understood with the following examples.

▶ **GR/IR Clearing Sample Scenario One**:
  1. A purchase order is sent to the vendor for 100 items at €1 each.
  2. The vendor sends a partial delivery of 50 pieces.
  3. Upon receipt, a posting is made of €50 to the stock account for the 50 pieces received, and a balancing entry of €50 (negative) is posted to the GR/IR clearing account. The transaction therefore balances.
  4. The GR/IR clearing account now shows that you need to keep €50 available to pay an invoice that is likely to arrive in the near future for the 50 pieces received.
  5. The vendor then sends in an invoice for €50 for the 50 pieces that were delivered.
  6. When the invoice is entered, it will post a balancing entry of 50 pieces at the goods-receipt value (€50) to the GR/IR clearing account, regardless of the invoice value. This clears the account.
  7. In this scenario, €50 was posted to the clearing account with the opposing €50 (negative) being posted to the vendor account as a debt to be paid.
  8. The end result is a zero balance on the GR/IR clearing account indicating that all receipts now have been paid for.

▶ **GR/IR Clearing Sample Scenario Two**:
  1. A purchase order is sent to the vendor for 100 items at €1 each.
  2. The vendor sends a partial delivery of 50 pieces.
  3. Upon receipt, a posting is made of €50 to the stock account for the 50 pieces received and a balancing entry of €50 (negative) is posted to the GR/IR clearing account. The transaction therefore balances.
  4. The GR/IR clearing account now shows that you need to keep €50 available to pay for an invoice that is likely to arrive in the near future for the 50 pieces received. So far, this is the same as in the first scenario.
  5. This time, the vendor sends in an invoice for €100 for 100 pieces (the full amount, even though only half of the order has been received).

6. When the invoice is entered, it will post an entry of 100 pieces totaling € 100 (based on the goods receipt value of € 1 each) to the clearing account. The invoice will be blocked from payment because the remaining 50 pieces have not yet been received.
7. The end result of the invoice entry is a balance of € 50 for 50 items on the GR/IR clearing account, and this will remain there until we receive the remaining 50 pieces (or manually balance this by using a special clearing entry). The clearing account therefore indicates that we have paid for some materials that we have not yet received.

▶ **GR/IR Clearing Sample Scenario Three:**
1. A purchase order is sent to the vendor for 100 items at € 1 each.
2. The vendor sends the first 50 pieces.
3. Upon receipt, a posting of € 50 is made to the stock account for the 50 pieces received, and a balancing entry of € 50 (negative) is posted to the GR/IR clearing account. The transaction therefore balances.
4. The GR/IR clearing account now shows that you need to keep € 50 available to pay for an invoice that is likely to arrive in the near future for the 50 pieces received. To this point, the situation is the same as in the first scenario.
5. The vendor sends an invoice for € 25 for 25 pieces (less than the delivered amount), and this may be an error by the vendor.
6. When the invoice is entered, it will post a balancing entry of 25 pieces at the GR value (regardless of the invoice value) of € 25. The invoice will be cleared for payment because it is for less than the value we owe the vendor.
7. The end result is a balance of € 25 (negative) for 25 items on the GR/IR account. This will remain there until we receive an invoice for the remaining 25 pieces.

▶ **GR/IR Clearing Sample Scenario Four:**
1. A purchase order is sent to the vendor for 100 items at € 1 each.
2. The vendor sends the first 50 pieces.
3. Upon receipt, a posting of € 50 is made to the stock account for the 50 pieces received, and a balancing entry of € 50 (negative) is posted to the GR/IR clearing account. The transaction therefore balances.
4. The GR/IR clearing account now shows that we need to keep € 50 available to pay for an invoice that is likely to arrive in the near future for the 50 pieces received. So far, this is the same as in the first scenario.
5. The vendor sends an invoice for € 75 for 50 pieces. Again, this may be an error by the vendor.
6. When we enter the invoice, it will post a balancing entry of 50 pieces at the GR value (regardless of the invoice value) of € 50 to the clearing account. The invoice will be blocked for payment because of the price difference.
7. The end result is a zero balance on the GR/IR clearing account even though the vendor has charged more than we expected. The reason: We were expecting an invoice for 50 pieces, and we now have an invoice for 50 pieces, so there is no balance to account for.

Using MR11 to Manage the GR/IR Clearing Account

Transaction MR11 is designed to be used to view or manage the GR/IR clearing account. This function is normally the responsibility of the finance department, but it needs help from the purchasing and inventory departments to determine whether the balance should be cleared or left for future action, such as a goods receipt or credit note. It is quite possible that a vendor has delivered items and not yet invoiced for them for technical reasons, and so the delay may not actually indicate that the vendor will not send in an invoice. Figure 3.1 shows the initial selection screen.

This transaction is used for two main purposes:

▶ As a report to show the current situation relating to invoices and goods receipts that have not yet been matched
▶ As a clearing transaction to balance out the entries and resolve discrepancies when the invoice is not going to be sent or the goods are not going to arrive

Use the main selection options in the **Document Header Data** and **Choose** sections, to narrow the entries to those that you wish to deal with. Many of the options available

3   Financial Aspects of Invoice Verification

Figure 3.1 MR11 Selection Screen for GR/IR Clearing Account

in the other fields on the selection screen have very specific uses.

The clearing account is designed to show the value of non-invoiced receipts or invoices with no receipts. The selection options therefore include the flags to show either or both of these alternatives, which are shown in Figure 3.1 in the **Surplus Types** section.

If you select **Delivery surplus**, you will only see those deliveries (i.e., receipts) that have not yet been invoiced. If you select **Invoice surplus**, you will only see those invoices for which a full receipt has not yet been posted. You can select both fields if you wish. This is ideal when you want to see the total balance of the account.

The **Clear section** indicates which clearing accounts you wish to work with. You can choose the **GR/IR**, **Freight**, or **ERS** clearing accounts. Note that with release ERP 6 — shown here — you get the separate option of **ERS Purchase Orders** and **ERS Delivery costs** instead of one flag for **ERS**.

The final three fields at the bottom of the **Choose** section allow you to control the records to be displayed, depending on the size of the imbalance. This setting can be used to clear old records that are for small variances.

These small variances could take a lot of effort to clear for little benefit. If the difference is very small and also very old, you can normally assume that it can be cleared automatically. For instance, if an invoice was received six months ago for bulk materials, and the invoice quantity was for 9.875 tons, and the goods receipt was posted for 9.800 tons, then it would be safe to assume that the vendor is unlikely to deliver the missing 0.075th of a ton six months later.

You can use these settings to indicate the age of the items and the allowed variances that you want to view or to clear automatically. Let's look at examples of the entries made to the three fields.

- The **Last movement before key date** field could be set to a date six months earlier. This means that the system will not consider anything that has had an invoice, credit memo, or receipt posted in the last six months. This way, you can assume that the purchase order and invoice are to be classed as fully processed.
- The **Qty Var. Less Than/Equal To** field is used to limit the size of item to be cleared. Set this at a very low percentage initially, and then increase it gradually for each run, so that you can be sure that the records being cleared represent only small differences. An initial setting of 2% to start with, rising to 10%, is normal. But the percentage used should be in line with the **Last movement before key date** field. This is important, because a small percentage on an invoice posted six months ago may be cleared without major risk, but the same percentage on an invoice posted only last month may be premature.
- The **Value Variance Less Than/= To** field is used in conjunction with the percentage to ensure that you do not clear large values just because they are a small percentage of a high-value invoice.

> **Note:** If you just want to view all entries in the clearing account, enter maximum percentages and values in these fields and ensure that the purchase order dates, etc., are broad enough to capture the required entries.

The **Processing** window controls whether the transaction is being run as a report or an update. The **Prepare list** flag must always be set *on* if you just want to view the entries. Setting the **Automatic clearance** flag on will clear all entries that match the selection criteria (taking the percentages and values into consideration). The **Layout** field allows you to specify a previously saved layout instead of the standard default layout.

Regular Maintenance of the Clearing Accounts

The clearing accounts should be maintained regularly, at least monthly. If they are not, the contents of the account will quickly become unmanageable and genuine problems may go unnoticed (that is, until the vendor notices them).

We recommend running the automatic clearing with a date of six or so months ago for a percentage of 5% to 10% and a value of less than € 20 (but this depends entirely on your own approach to these discrepancies). This should clear all of the simple variances where the cost of investigating them far outweighs the cost of clearing them in this way.

Once this is done, you should run the transaction again but this time as a report. This is more likely to leave you with genuine discrepancies that need to be examined in more detail. You then can investigate any suspicious entries and either chase the receipt of the stock or invoice (whichever is overdue) or manually clear the entry, if appropriate. You can clear manually by selecting the record and clicking on the **Post** button, as shown in Figure 3.2.

Figure 3.2 Detailed Display of MR11

The overall result of a clearing, whether done manually or automatically, is to indicate that the outstanding invoice or receipt is not likely to happen. The system will then base its financial postings on any invoiced quantity being used to value a receipt that has been posted.

For example, if there has been a receipt of 100 items at € 10 each, the stock account was updated with a value of € 1,000 when the receipt was posted. If an invoice is received but the quantity invoiced was 90 and the difference is cleared with transaction MR11, then a negative value of € 100 will be posted to the consumption account or stock account — provided the item is moving-average-price (MAP) controlled — whichever is relevant to the PO. There will be a posting to a price-variance account if the item was posted to stock and is standard-price controlled. These postings occur because this is now the true cost of the items received and so the previous postings have to be updated.

The clearing values are stored on the clearing document for enquiry and audit-trail purposes. Everything now balances, and this entry is cleared from the MR11 report. You would still have to clear the items against each other financially using transaction F.13 or transaction F13E, but from a SAP Invoice Verification aspect the items are no longer unbalanced.

The GR/IR clearing account can often become more complicated than it needs to be. This can happen if invoices are being posted against the wrong purchase orders. Worse still, a purchase order may have been created deliberately to match an invoice that has been received when a purchase order already existed was not used to match to the invoice because it couldn't be traced. This results in the original purchase order being left on the clearing account with no invoice to clear it against, assuming there was a receipt posted against it.

In such a case, you should reverse the invoice, reverse the purchase order that was specially created to match the invoice and then rematch the invoice with the correct PO. You have the option of just clearing the original order using transaction MR11. While this might appear to work, you will have had two receipts posted, both with a value, and so your financial postings are now incorrect.

Transaction MR11SHOW can be used to display or cancel a clearing document that has been created via transaction MR11. MR11SHOW is not (as its name would suggest) a display-only version of MR11.

3.4 Tax Processing Within Invoice Verification

Different countries have different tax rules and procedures, so you need to ensure that your company codes have been assigned to the correct tax procedures when they were configured. In general, this is a procedure such as TAXGB for taxes in Great Britain. This will allow appropriate tax codes to be maintained with the correct percentages. These are:

- V1—VAT at 17.5%
- V0—VAT at 0%

These codes can be entered on the purchase order item line (**Invoice** tab), as shown in Figure 3.3.

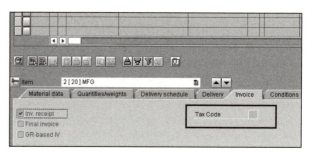

Figure 3.3 Tax Code Field on Purchase Order Item (Invoice Tab)

This entry is not mandatory (except for ERS orders, described in Section 2.4). This means that the VAT code may be blank on the PO item line. This means that in the transaction MIRO invoice verification screen you will need to specify the relevant code or, at the very least, set up default codes in configuration (see Section 4.5). The tax code can also be specified on the **Basic data** tab of the MIRO transaction, or it can be left blank, especially if there are multiple codes on the purchase order. The tax code on the basic data tab applies to the invoice at the header level. Figure 3.4 shows the tax-code field on the MIRO **Basic data** tab.

Figure 3.4 Tax Code Field on MIRO Basic Data Tab

> **Note:** If you need to use different tax codes for the same item on a purchase order, always use a different order-item line for each tax code. Within MIRO, you cannot have the same order-item line repeated in the line-item display. Thus, you will not be able to specify two different tax codes for the same item.

The Calculate Tax Flag

You have the option of flagging the **Calculate tax** box to indicate that you want the system to calculate the tax that applies to this invoice. This is shown in Figure 3.4.

> **Note:** The **Amount** field on the same tab must always include any taxes. The tax-amount field should contain the portion of the total invoice amount that is tax. Alternatively, you should set **Calculate tax** to have this calculated automatically based on the tax codes specified.

There is no right or wrong setting of the **Calculate tax** field; the end result is the same either way. However, we recommend that you do not set **Calculate tax** but rather enter the tax amount manually. By doing this, you are getting the system to check the tax calculation that the vendor has specified on the invoice. If you merely check **Calculate tax** each time, you may miss the fact that the vendor's calculations are different. This may occur because the **Manage small differences** tolerance settings are accepting the differences as small rounding errors each time.

By manually keying the tax amount specified by the vendor, you are fully checking the invoice and tax amounts. For example, if the vendor undercharged you by a small amount for the items on the invoice and somehow managed to overcharge you for the tax by the same amount, you need to capture this information correctly. If you have **Calculate tax** checked, the invoice may balance when it shouldn't. With the field left blank, the system will highlight the price differences and the incorrect tax calculation, even when they cancel each other out.

The Tax Tab in the MIRO Transaction

If you select the **Tax** tab within the MIRO transaction, you will be able to see and/or maintain the different tax codes that are relevant to this invoice and the tax values against each code. This is especially useful if you have an invoice with multiple tax codes. Figure 3.5 shows the detail available on the **Tax** tab

Figure 3.5 Tax Tab Details

You can change the **Calculate tax** field in this tab if required. You can enter, delete, or change values against each tax code, and you can view the effect on the tax values of posting the invoice net (i.e., net of cash discounts, covered in Section 4.5), by clicking on the **Net proposal** button.

3.5 Moving Average Price/Standard Price

The price control (on the **Accounting** view of the material master record) is an important setting and can dramatically influence the way that values in goods receipts and invoice receipts are posted. You can use different methods for different materials, or you can decide to have the same price control used for all materials. Which option to use is often decided by a personal preference within the finance department, based on previous experience, but it can also depend on how variable your purchase prices are.

If your prices are relatively static and predictable, then standard pricing can sometimes be more appropriate. This is because there are fewer postings to the price-variance account, and so there are fewer corrections to manage.

MAP control tends to be more appropriate if the purchase prices vary more frequently. In such cases, fewer price variances will be posted, and the MAP is more likely to reflect the true costs of the items because all costs are posted to the stock account. In contrast, standard-price-controlled materials only post the standard price to the stock account.

It is important to realize that values are sometimes posted to the stock account when an invoice is posted. This only happens if you are using the MAP control and the invoice values cause adjustments due to different prices or when additional cost — such as delivery costs — are entered at invoice stage.

The Difference Between Standard Pricing and MAP

There is one main difference between the two options. With standard pricing, any posting to or from the stock account will always be at the standard price regardless of the actual values involved. With MAP, all values that can be attributed to the cost of the item will be posted to the stock account. The price is then averaged out against the value of existing stock, and when an item is issued it will always be at the relevant MAP.

Advantages of Each Option

Which option is best depends on many factors, and what is classed as an advantage by one person could be seen as a disadvantage by another.

For example, one perceived advantage of standard pricing is that the value used at consumption or goods-issue stage remains constant. This can help with budgeting because every department will have the same costs associated with consumption.

On the other hand, the standard price is sometimes only set once or twice a year and so it is unlikely to be correct all year long, especially if the prices vary throughout the year. This situation may result in every posting using an incorrect value, so that the profit-and-loss data on the movements of these items is likely to be misleading.

The differences caused by this will be stored in a price-variance account, and this will need to be managed so that the actual costs are reflected correctly in the profit-and-loss statements.

If you use MAP, one perceived advantage is that the consumption values will be based on an average of the actual costs of the material, and so they are more likely to be a fair assumption of cost. But if two items are consumed at different times and therefore at potentially two different values, should one posted cost be very different from another for exactly the same material? If two different departments are using the same materials for similar purposes and are being charged at different prices, at least one department may feel that this is unfair.

Let's look at an example that illustrates the main differences between the two options and shows some of the advantages and disadvantages of each option.

▶ We start with two items in stock, one purchased at a cost of € 100 (perhaps part of a special deal) and the other for € 500 (perhaps it was purchased from a different and more expensive vendor for some reason). The production department wants to use one of the items as a component.

▶ If MAP control is used, the MAP would be set by the system at € 300 (100 plus 500, divided by two) and there would be € 600 in the stock account. The € 300 MAP could be seen to be a reasonable cost price to use, even though we have never actually purchased one of these items at € 300. The production-planning department will be charged € 300, and if anyone else was to use the remaining item they too would be charged € 300. The total cost of purchasing has therefore been passed on to the departments that have used the items.

▶ If standard price control is used, the standard price will have been set manually (for the sake of this example) at € 200, probably because it was believed that this would be a reasonable price to pay for this item. The stock account would contain only € 400 in total (the receipts, as with every posting, were at the standard price regardless of the purchase costs). The first receipt would have posted a negative € 100 to the price-variance account and € 200 (the standard price) to the stock account (a total of € 100 to match the actual costs). The second receipt would have posted a positive € 300 to the price variance account and € 200 (the standard price) to the stock account. That results in a total of € 500 to match the actual costs.

- The production department would be charged € 200, and if anyone else was to use the other item they too would be charged € 200. The stock account would now be zero (as it was with the MAP option), but the total charged for the use of the items is only € 400. There is still € 200 in the price variance account: The negative € 100 for the first receipt and the € 300 from the second receipt.

Both options use accepted financial postings, and so the choice depends on which is most appropriate for the situation involved.

Although the above example focuses on the postings caused by goods receipts and issues, the concept is the same during invoice verification. In this case, if there are any postings that affect stock accounts, the system will use the above rules to determine whether that posting should be made directly to or from the stock account (for MAP materials) or to or from the price-variance account (for standard-priced materials).

3.6 Payment Run

This process can be automated, but many businesses prefer to retain manual control over what gets paid and when. The payment run is a standard SAP transaction that works on line or scheduled as a batch job. The transaction is F110, or you can use transaction F110S to schedule the payment run at set intervals. Figure 3.6 shows the initial screen of transaction F110 and the tabs that are available.

Figure 3.6 Initial Screen of Transaction F110: Payment Run

The initial screen is used to give the payment run a unique reference and to capture the payment-run date. Indicate the date of the payment run and specify an identification code (up to five characters). This code will be used to identify the result of the run later. Fill out the remainder of the selections on the four tabs available.

Parameter Tab

The parameter tab section is used to control which items are paid. It enables you to select certain company codes, payment methods, vendors, and/or customers. In implementations that use multiple companies, each company can still control when and who they pay. Figure 3.7 shows the **Parameter** tab fields.

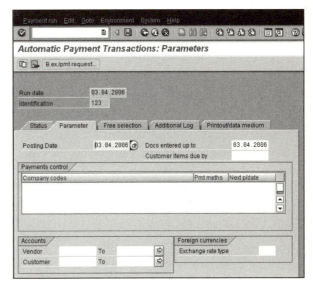

Figure 3.7 Parameter Tab Fields

Select the company code or codes that you wish to include in the payment run. If you are entering more than one company code, enter each code followed by a comma and then the next company code (no spaces). You can enter a range or ranges of company codes by using the format 0001, 0006, which in this case indicates all company codes from 0001 to 0006 inclusive.

Indicate the payment methods you want to process (check, BACS, etc.) by entering the single letter code or codes, again without spaces and this time with no commas. Note that all documents that match the selections made will be included in the payment run. If a document has a payment method that is not included here, it will not be paid, and it will appear in the list of exceptions.

You must enter the date of the next payment run so that the program can select the correct payments to make. This field ensures that you pay your vendors at the latest possible moment without losing discounts and without missing deadlines. The program simply uses this date to determine whether any deadline for payment (or discount) will be missed if the payment is left until the next payment run. This means that you can run the payment program regularly without paying too early. We recommend running the payment program frequently so that dates are not missed.

Running the program infrequently will also result in payments being made too early. Here are some examples:

- If you only run the payment program once every month, and a vendor gives you 14 days to pay, the invoice will be paid early. The reason: It will be paid in the current run because if it isn't, the next payment run will be too late. In fact, the payment will be made up to 14 days early depending on the date of the run.
- If you run the payment program weekly (or even daily), you are less likely to pay an invoice early, because the program will determine that there is another chance to pay the invoice later and so it can wait until a future payment run.
- If you decide to run the payment program infrequently, then you may need to trick the system into thinking that the next payment run will be earlier than it is by entering a date for the next run as early as the next day. This will prevent items from being paid early, but you will miss deadlines for payment for many items.

Enter a range or list of vendors or customers you want to include in the payment run. Use the range 1 to ZZZZZZZZZZ if you wish to include all partners.

Enter an exchange rate type if you do not wish to use the default average rate (rate type **M**).

The Free Selection Tab

The free-selection tab provides you with a flexible range of fields that can be used to include or exclude items due for payment. This is especially useful if you need to use specific fields related to the document, vendor, or customer. Figure 3.8 shows the **Free selection** tab fields.

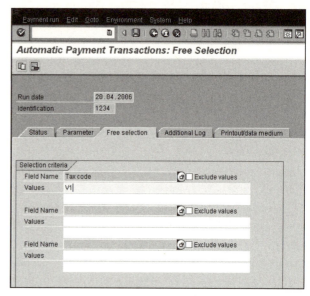

Figure 3.8 Free-Selection Tab Fields

You can enter values for selected fields that you wish to include or exclude in the run.

Select the source of the required field (**Document**, **Vendor**, or **Customer**) from the pull-down list, select the appropriate field from the list displayed, then enter the values and or ranges to be excluded or included (depending on the **Exclude values** flag).

The Additional Log tab

This is not relevant to payment runs in an established SAP system. It is only used in the early days of an implementation when full payment logs are required to verify what has happened in detail. This detail is normally not required or adds no value once the payment has worked as expected. Figure 3.9 shows the **Additional Log** tab fields.

This tab is normally left blank during payment runs. It can be used in early or test runs to provide a log of the actions that took place during the run. You can decide what you want to see in this log by selecting the appropriate flags and indicating any specific vendors or customers.

3.6 Payment Run

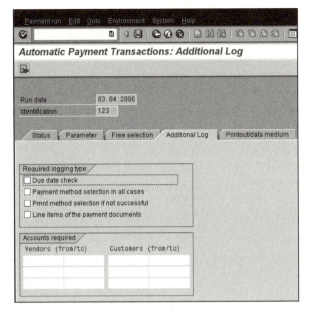

Figure 3.9 Additional Log Tab Fields

The Printout/Data Medium Tab
Figure 3.10 shows the **Printout/data medium** tab fields.

Figure 3.10 Printout/Data Medium Tab Fields

You can indicate the variant to be used for the appropriate print program for payment documents and other items. You can also select the list and variant to be used for the log and summary reports.

Running F110
To execute the payment run with transaction F110, you must save the entries first. We advise saving different variants for each run so you don't to enter all details each time. When you have saved the details, the status screen will be displayed.

You can then either run the transaction as a full payment run or as a proposal run. The latter enables you to calculate who will be paid and what the total value will be without actually making payment. When the program is executed, you can view the progress from the status tab, it will show the status as each stage is completed.

The F110S Transaction
This has the same fields and options as the F110 transaction but is designed to be used when scheduling the payment run as a batch job. All the fields are on one screen and can be saved as a variant. Make sure that you check the **Proposal** box if you wish to see the proposed payments rather than a full payment run. Figure 3.11 shows the transaction F110S screen.

Figure 3.11 Transaction F110S Screen

www.sap-press.com 59

3.7 Summary

Although this chapter focuses on the financial aspects of invoice verification, this process should not be handled by the financial team alone. The materials-management team must be involved in the financial design. Some implementations miss this vital point, and the result is a function that operates correctly from a financial point of view but does not operate efficiently or simply from a user viewpoint.

4 Configuration

This chapter covers the configuration options available within SAP Invoice Verification. This is not merely a case of knowing what to configure. It is vitally important to know the effects of the many configuration options. Some options are quite simple, and the settings are obvious. Others sometimes appear unimportant or irrelevant, and yet they can sometimes make a huge difference to the functionality available. This chapter will focus largely on the less obvious areas of configuration.

We strongly recommend that you read the ample text help that SAP provides on each configuration step. The help text icon is found on each configuration menu option, as shown in Figure 4.1.

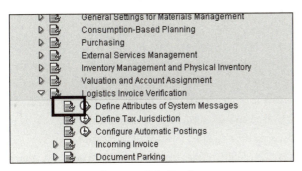

Figure 4.1 SAP Configuration Help-Text Icon

With a few exceptions, this help text is very useful and can sometimes help just by confirming what you already believed about the configuration step for which it was meant to be used.

Although every step is covered within this chapter, extra time will be spent on the more complex options and in particular on those that can unlock extra functionality. By following this guide and confirming your assumptions with the help text available, you should be able to tackle the configuration of Invoice Verification with confidence and provide users with a flexible, efficient, and user-friendly process.

4.1 Basic Configuration

We recommend carrying out the configuration via the main transaction SPRO. There are individual transactions for many configuration options, but by using these you can sometimes miss out on additional options. By using SPRO and drilling down through the menus, you will follow the basic configuration in the sequence that SAP recommends. In addition, you will be able to view the help documentation at each level.

The SPRO transaction will look similar to that shown in Figure 4.2, depending on which version of SAP you are using.

In all the following examples, we assume that you will use the **SAP Reference Implementation Guide (IMG) option**. This option shows all of the configuration steps. If your implementation is using IMG Projects, you may need to select the appropriate project from the list. The options available within a project IMG are normally restricted to those relevant to the implementation. Thus, by using the SAP Reference IMG at this point, every option will be included.

Figure 4.3 shows the expanded configuration menu. It is worth noting that Invoice Verification is referred to as Logistics Invoice Verification. You will find this within the Materials Management configuration menu (not the Financial Accounting menu as you might expect).

Note that the Invoice Verification configuration is split down into several sections. The standard SAP approach is to have the structure of the menus set up so that you start at the top and work your way down. This is only a very rough guide. As you can see from the sequence here — starting with **Define Attributes of System Messages** as the first option — it is not a hard and fast rule.

4 Configuration

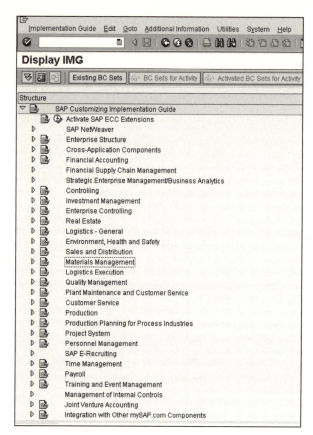

Figure 4.2 SPRO Transaction Initial Screen

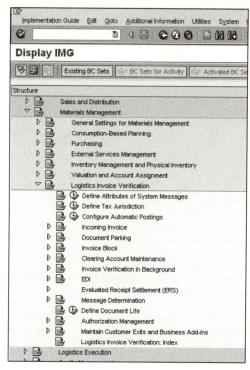

Figure 4.3 Standard SAP Menu List for Invoice Verification

Each of the configuration options will be covered in the sequence they appear in the standard SAP menu list for Invoice Verification, shown in Figure 4.3.

The first three menu options — **Define Attributes of System Messages**, **Define Tax Jurisdiction**, and **Configure Automatic Postings** — are not sub-menus, as such; they are single configuration steps. They do not affect a specific area in Invoice Verification, but are more general and so are not contained within the more specific sub-menus.

4.2 Define the Attributes of System Messages

This is a powerful configuration option, and yet many implementations overlook its benefits. It can be used to control many of the messages that are displayed during invoice verification. A message can be set as an error message to stop any further processing. It also can be set as a warning message and so allow the user to continue, or it can be set *off* so that the message is not displayed.

However, switching off a message in this manner does not always work. Some errors cannot be switched off because the program logic would not be able to continue without the error being corrected. The fact that you can configure the message to be switched off does not mean it will not be set to an error by the program. Apart from these exceptions, setting the messages to error and warnings according to your needs is often essential.

Another control that can be a real benefit is the ability to control individual messages by **User Name**. This can result in one user getting an error message and being prevented from continuing while another user gets a warning message and is allowed to continue.

This capability can be useful when you want certain messages to prevent a standard user from continuing — for instance when a large change is made to the Moving Average Price (MAP) — but you want the supervisor to be able to process the invoice if need be. If you were to merely set the error message to stop further processing, then nobody could continue. But by setting the message as an error message for all standard users and then setting it as a warning message for the supervisor or supervisors, you achieve flexibility in processing.

You also may need to set messages differently for batch runs than you do for online runs of the same transaction. Often there is little point in having any warning messages in the batch run because the update will need to continue anyway.

Moreover, you may wish to change messages that are normally warnings to full error messages to stop the batch run, because you have no way of making a decision based on that message. Whatever the reason, being able to set different types of messages for batch runs is often essential.

How to Configure System Messages

If you want to have all of the standard messages unchanged, then you need do nothing. If you leave the table empty, the standard defaults for each message will be used.

If you want to control a message, you will need to find the relevant message number. This can be obtained from the pull-down list of message numbers, as shown in Figure 4.4, or by double-clicking on any message when it is displayed.

You add the selected message as a new entry by clicking on the **New Entries** icon and pressing Enter, or by selecting the appropriate message number; the message text and the standard settings will be filled in when you press Enter.

You then can change the flags. If you leave the **User Name** field blank, these settings will apply to all users. If you need different settings for different users, you need to have a separate entry for each.

Remember: If the standard message setting is to be used for some users, you only need entries for the users who will have a non-standard setting, because the table should contain only the exceptions from the standard set-

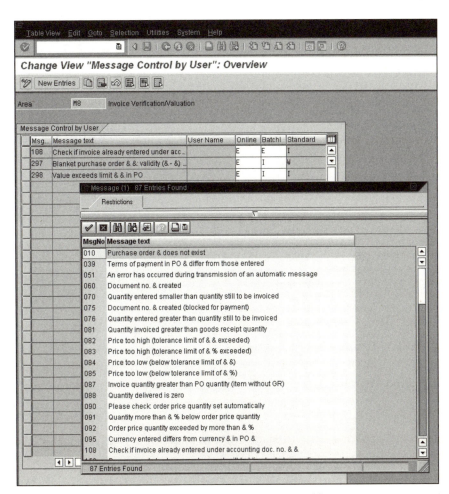

Figure 4.4 List of Messages from Pull-Down Option in Message Field

tings. If the standard setting for a message is an error, and you want a supervisor to be allowed to continue if he or she gets this message, then you only need to have one entry in the table with the supervisor's user name and the flag set to a warning message. Figure 4.5 shows an example of message settings.

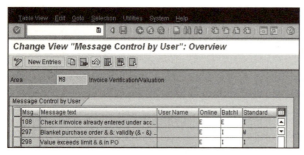

Figure 4.5 Three Messages Being Controlled

The effects of the settings on the three entries shown in the example in Figure 4.5 are as follows:

- Message 108 is normally set as an "information" message. It is not a warning, merely a message to inform the user of an event (it has an **I** in the **Standard** field). If this message is triggered in a batch job, then it will be treated as a serious error and the record will not be updated (it has an **E** in the **Batchl** field). If the message is triggered online, then it will have the standard information message (it has an **I** in the **Online** field). This message will be given the same setting for all users (the **User Name** field is blank).
- Message 297 is normally set as a warning message. The user will see a warning but will be allowed to continue (it has an **W** in the **Standard** field). If this message is triggered in a batch job, then it will be treated as an information message, and the record can be processed if the batch run allows this (it has an **I** in the **Batchl** field). If the message is triggered online, the user will see an error message and will not be allowed to continue until the error has been resolved (it has an **E** in the **Online** field). This message will be given the same setting for all users (the **User Name** field is blank).
- Message 298 normally is set as an information message (it has an **I** in the Standard field). If this message is triggered in a batch job, then it will again issue an information message (it has an **I** in the **Batchl** field). If the message is triggered online then it will have the stan-

dard information message (it has an **I** in the **Online** field). This message will be given the same setting for all users (the **User Name** field is blank).

It is normal to start with this table empty during the initial phases of design and only add entries as the design begins to take shape.

4.3 Define Tax Jurisdiction

You can be forgiven for thinking that there is a bug in the IMG when you first examine this configuration option. It is entitled **Define tax jurisdiction,** and yet when you open it you are taken to the configuration of plants.

This is not a bug. It is just that there is a setting on the configuration of plants that contains the tax jurisdiction data, and so this uses the same transaction.

You may not need to configure this data, because this configuration is designed for use in the United States only.

Select the **Plant** from the list and click on the **Details** icon (or double click on the **Plant** line). This will take you to the plant details screen shown in Figure 4.6.

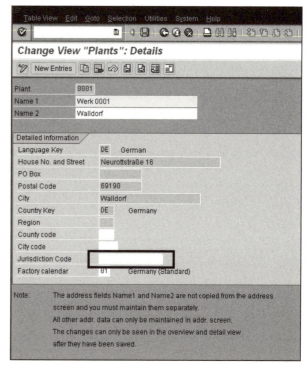

Figure 4.6 Plant Details Screen Showing the Jurisdiction Field

This field should always be set to the city where goods are supplied. This may be different from the address stored for the plant.

4.4 Configure Automatic Postings

The most important thing to realize about this configuration option is that you are not configuring the way the system carries out the accounting. You are merely specifying the general ledger (G/L) account numbers of the accounts that the system should use in specific predefined circumstances.

You can change to some extent the way that the system carries out its accounting processes, but this is rarely required and certainly not recommended.

The system has validated standard built-in accounting practices that are designed to match the rigid rules of accounting. Any changes to this could lead to problems. All you normally need to do is to specify the account numbers to be used for certain transactions such as goods receipt/invoice receipt (GR/IR) clearing, price variances, and freight provisions.

A combined team of materials management and finance staff normally carries out this configuration. Sometimes it is left to one or the other of these groups, with less-than-optimal results. The materials management team is normally responsible for the configuration of invoice verification, but team members often feel unqualified to make the financial decisions involved in this step.

However, if the process is merely handed over to the finance team, these people will not normally have been involved in the full invoice verification design, including the detailed processes that surround price variances, freight, and similar transactions. A combined team effort is the way to go.

There are three main sections within the configuration option:

- Account assignment
- Simulation
- G/L accounts

Each section is very different, so we should think of these as three separate configuration transactions. Of the three, only the account assignment option allows you to configure anything; the other two options are display transactions that can be used to help ensure that the settings are correct.

Account Assignment

This is the main configuration step in automatic account determination and is probably the most complex configuration in all of SAP. The terminology used does nothing to help simplify the process. The word "valuation" is used in many of the main entities involved (valuation area, valuation area group, valuation class, valuation modifier, etc.), and this adds to the confusion. A quick explanation of the main terms is essential before we dig into the details. These terms are:

- The valuation area, in almost all stock-based implementations, is simply the financial name for a plant. This means that in this case, whenever the term "valuation area" is used, you can safely substitute the word "plant" for it. In exceptional circumstances, the valuation area can be set to be the same as the company code, but this means that plants cannot be accounted for differently, because the company code is a level above the plant level.
- The valuation area group allows you to combine similar plants to remove the need to duplicate entries that apply across all plants. Typical groupings include all production facilities in one group, all warehouses in another, and non-stock plants in a final group. You also sometimes can find all plants grouped into one single valuation-area group.
- The valuation class is also a grouping function. It allows materials that are to be treated the same, for accounting purposes, to be grouped together. Typical valuation classes reflect the types of material involved, such as raw materials, finished products, or services. They often relate in some way to the material types, but this is not a requirement. Basically this class allows you to set automatic accounting by group (i.e., valuation class) rather than for each individual material.
- The valuation class is stored on the material master record (**Accounting** view), and possible entries are controlled by material type configuration. Figure 4.7 shows the **Valuation Class** field on the material master Accounting view.

4 Configuration

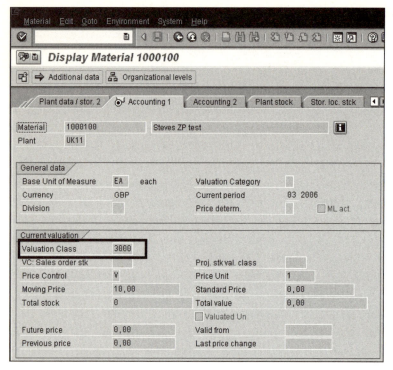

Figure 4.7 Valuation Class Field on Material Master Accounting View

The **transaction/event key** presents the biggest challenge to understanding the automated accounting terminology.

For each event in the process, there will be a key that allows you to set the account to be used for that event. Transaction/event keys can be added and changed, but this would be done rarely, and we definitely do not recommend the practice. It is best to work with the existing keys and treat them as if they are unchangeable. Typical examples are BSX, PRD, and WRX.

Once the terminology is understood, the real challenge begins. The process itself can appear to be a black box, but in fact depends on three basic pieces of information:

- What is happening?
- Where is it happening?
- What is it happening to?

The combination of these three facts determines which account is to be updated. If the same thing is happening in the same place to the same type of material, the account used will be the same, but if any of these factors differ the account used can be different. The three elements of the process can be thought of as follows:

- "What is happening" could be a posting to the GR/IR clearing account following the posting of an invoice relating to an item that has been received. This is the transaction/event key selected by the system that suits the action taking place.
- "Where is it happening" affects the account to be used if you have decided to treat different valuation areas (i.e., plants) differently.
- "What is it happening to" uses the valuation class to determine which account is to be updated.

The transaction/event key is derived from the SAP transaction. The valuation area (or valuation area group if used) is derived from the plant, and the valuation class is derived from the material.

During configuration, you now have to set up the correct G/L account number for each of the combinations of these three variables. Any combination that you don't use can be left alone as long as you are sure that this situation will never arise.

Figure 4.8 shows the first page of the list of **transaction/event keys** shown when you select **Account assignment** from the first screen of the automatic account determination configuration transaction.

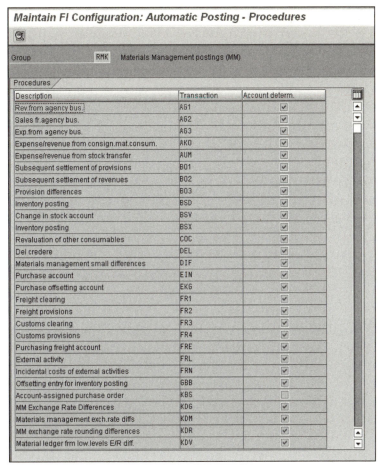

Figure 4.8 Transaction/Event Keys

To view or maintain the entries of a key:

- Double-click on the transaction/event key line.
- The system will ask you to enter the chart of accounts (COA) that you wish to work with. This only happens the first time you select a key; subsequently the system remembers the COA used previously.
- The next screen displayed will vary depending on how that key has been set up. Each key has associated "rules," and these determine how many variables can be used to affect the account used.
- To view or maintain the rules, click on the **Rules** function box on the accounts screen, as shown in Figure 4.9.

Up to four rules can be flagged, and the number of flags available is linked directly to the **transaction/event key**. The standard settings of these flags are often correct, but you may have to change the settings for some keys.

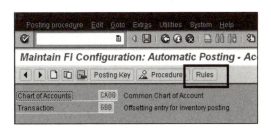

Figure 4.9 Rules Function Box

Note: Changing the rule flag on a transaction/event key will cause all entries to be removed from the configuration of that key. Only change the flags if you are sure that you want this to happen.

The four keys are as follows (see Figure 4.10):

- **Debit/Credit** — With this flag set off you will only have one field for the account number and so debits and credits will be posted to the same account. If you set this flag *on* you will have the ability to set a different account number for each. postings

- **General modification** — This controls the extra variable called the account modifier. This field is not relevant to invoice verification; it is used to indicate the movement type that was used.
- **Valuation modif.** — This flag controls the variable valuation area group (although you would never guess this by the name). Set this *off*, and all postings to this event key will use the same account even if different plants are involved. Set it *on* and you can specify different accounts for each valuation area group that you have configured.
- **Valuation class** — Set this *on* if you want the account to depend on the valuation class of the material involved.

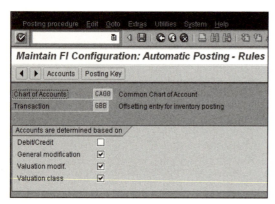

Figure 4.10 Four Rules Available on Each Transaction/Event Key

Some keys will have all rules switched off. These are rules that involve postings where the account is not determined by the plant or material involved and where the same account is used for debit and credit postings.

One such key is the WRX transaction/event key. This is used for postings to the GR/IR Clearing account. In this case, the main use of a clearing account is to collect all postings in the same account so they can be cleared against each other. Thus, it is not normal to have multiple accounts.

Figure 4.11 shows the **Maintain FI Configuration: Automatic Posting—Accounts** screen of the WRX key, where the only setting available is the G/L account number to be used.

Other keys may have all four flags set *on*. This will enable a different account to be specified for each scenario in a large combination of scenarios. This is normally used only for materials management postings such as goods issues, where the movement type (via the account modifier), the plant (via the valuation area/group), and the material (via the valuation class) all have an influence on the account used. The fourth flag sets the option of separate debit and credit accounts.

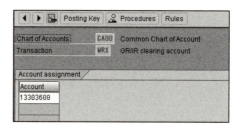

Figure 4.11 GR/IR Clearing Account Configuration Showing Only Account Number Entry

There is no easy way to ensure that you process each transaction/event key. You have to configure each one that is relevant to your implementation, and there are no safe short cuts to this process. It is much better to configure a key that may never be used than to miss one and find out during operation that this has been missed.

The other two main options in account determination, **Simulation** and **G/L accounts**, are very useful for checking that the account configuration is complete and correct.

Simulation

This function is also available within account determination, where it is used to simulate postings in order to verify which accounts will be used and to help determine if everything has been configured correctly. Figure 4.12 shows the function box to select to enter the simulation mode.

Figure 4.12 Simulation Function Box

The first time you use simulation, check the settings before you start. Select **Options** from the menu, and make the following settings for each of the following three options:

- Application area — This should be set to **Simulation** for invoice verification transactions.
- Input mode — This should ideally be set to **Input of Valuation Class** so that you do not have to specify a material number. You may wish to set to **Input of Material Number** if you prefer to specify a material number instead, but this does rely on that material number existing with an accounting view.
- Account check — This should be set to **Check of Referenced G/L Accounts** unless you have not yet set up the general-ledger account master data.

When the simulation screen appears, enter the **Plant** (so that the system can determine the valuation area or group), the **Material** (or valuation class) and then select the scenario you wish to simulate (so that the system can determine the transaction/event keys that apply). Figure 4.13 shows the simulation-screen selection options.

The system will display the results of the simulation. The header will show the organization details, and the system will have determined the company code, chart of accounts, valuation area, and valuation area group, all from the plant you specified.

Each potential posting will be displayed, but this does not mean that every posting will occur. The system is just showing every posting that is possible, depending on the circumstances involved (e.g., standard price or MAP, material-specified or not relevant.).

Each G/L account that has been determined will be displayed. If the G/L account field indicates a missing entry, this does not necessarily mean that anything is wrong. It just means that if that particular combination of events occurs no account can be determined. It may well be that this combination of events will never happen in your implementation, and so missing entries are not always errors.

The **AM** field shows the account modifier if applicable. For almost all invoice verification simulations, this will show **-e-**, meaning that no modifier applies. Figure 4.14 shows a sample simulation.

Use the simulation whenever you need to check the settings and don't necessarily want to create purchase orders, goods receipts, and invoice verification postings.

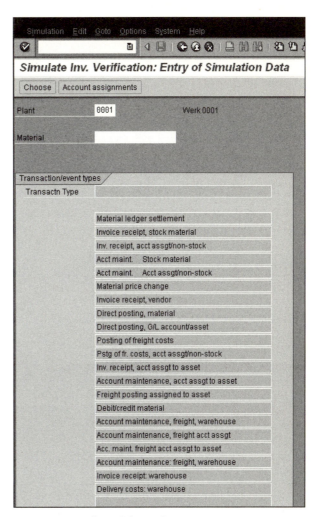

Figure 4.13 Simulation Selection Screen

Figure 4.14 Example of Simulation Screen

4 Configuration

G/L Accounts Function

We consider this a hidden gem of a function. It will display all of the accounts that will be posted to via automatic account determination, and it also will show under what circumstances those accounts are posted to. It can be run at any stage and provides a report designed to help the accounting department determine if the correct accounts are being used.

You merely enter the company code or valuation area (plant), and the system will list the accounts used. Figure 4.15 shows where the function can be triggered. Figure 4.16 shows an example of a result.

Figure 4.15 G/L Accounts Function Box

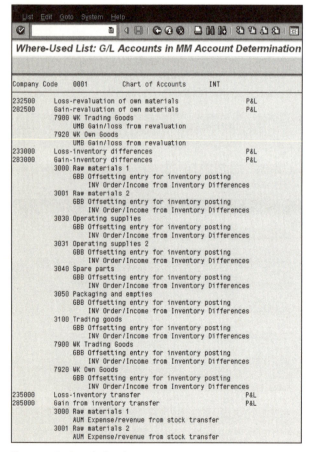

Figure 4.16 Sample Result

4.5 Incoming Invoice

This section of the configuration menu controls the settings that affect the posting of an invoice within the invoice verification transaction. The only exception is the control of the blocking of invoices for payment. A configuration for this is contained in a separate section of the menu. Figure 4.17 shows the contents of the **Incoming Invoice** section of the configuration menu.

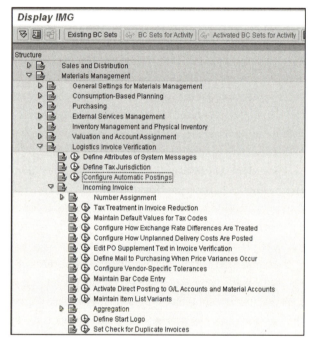

Figure 4.17 Incoming Invoice Configuration Sub-Menu

Number Assignment

There are two separate sections to this function:

▶ **Maintain Number Assignments for Accounting Documents**

 ▶ This section includes the number assignments and document types for all accounting documents (RE and RN being the two main invoice document types). Within this transaction, you can allocate number ranges and configure document types. We advise retaining and using the standard document types and number ranges provided by the system.

▶ **Maintain Number Assignment for Logistics Documents**

This is broken down to two further options:

- **Transaction—Assign Number Range,** in which the internal document types are linked to a number range ID. Here, too, we recommend leaving these as standard.
- **Maintain Number Range Intervals for Invoice Documents**, which allows you to manage the number ranges. This also can be maintained in the **Maintain Number Assignments for Accounting Documents** option.

Although the **Maintain Number Assignments for Accounting Documents** configuration option appears to deal only with number ranges, it also allows you to configure the document types. There are two main document types used in invoice verification. These are:

- RE
- RN

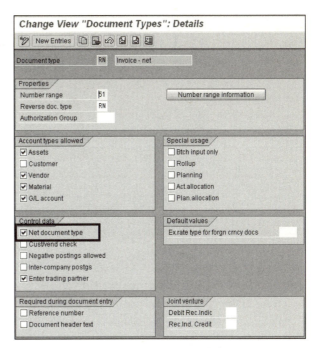

Figure 4.18 RN Document Type and Related Flag

The difference between the two main document types concerns the way that cash discounts (for prompt payment) are handled.

If you choose to use RN (net), any discounts that are relevant to the payment terms associated to the invoice will be assumed to be applicable, and the total payment to the vendor will be reduced by the discount due.

Choosing **RE** (Gross), the more commonly used document type, will post the full value as due to the vendor, and the discounts will be calculated as part of the payment run. They will be applied only if they are due according to the payment terms and the actual payment date. Figure 4.18 shows the **RN** document type and the flag that controls the calculation.

Tax Treatment in Invoice Reduction

This configuration option determines where the tax correction is applied when invoice reduction is involved. Refer to Section 2.5 for details of this functionality.

You can post the tax correction on the original document; that is, you can have the correct tax posted against the erroneous invoice with no tax in the credit note.

Alternatively, you can have the incorrect tax value posted in the original document, to match the incorrect invoice value. In the latter case, a correction tax can be posted in the complaint document, which is the automatic credit note created during invoice reduction.

There is no major advantage to doing this one way or the other, but if you normally have the system calculate taxes automatically it is often better to use the tax correction in the original document setting. The setting can be different for each company code used. Figure 4.19 shows the configuration screen.

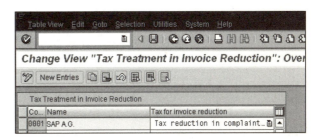

Figure 4.19 Tax Treatment in Invoice Reduction Screen

Maintain Default Values for Tax Codes

This configuration option controls which tax code is proposed by the system when an invoice is posted. It also controls which tax code is proposed by the system when unplanned delivery costs are posted. Figure 4.20 shows the configuration screen used to set the default tax codes.

4 Configuration

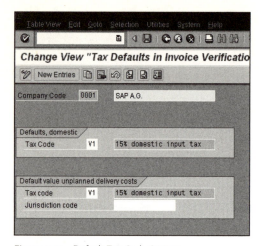

Figure 4.20 Default Tax Code Setting

Configure Treatment of Exchange-Rate Differences

Two main options are available from which to choose:

▶ You can treat exchange rate differences as such.
▶ You can treat them the same as any other price variance.

If you choose to treat them as exchange rate differences, you have two different ways to control exactly how the difference is calculated. These are:

▶ Determining the difference between the exchange rate at the time of goods receipt and the exchange rate at the time of invoice verification.
▶ Determining the difference between the exchange rate at the time of invoice verification and an assumed or budget exchange rate.

You specify in the configuration settings which exchange rate stored on the exchange rate table is to be used in the calculation (in the **ERT** field). Figure 4.21 shows the configuration screen.

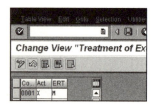

Figure 4.21 Exchange Rate Configuration Screen

Configure Posting of Unplanned Delivery Costs

When you add unplanned delivery costs to an invoice during invoice verification (see Section 2.2), you can handle these in two different ways. The system either can spread the costs among the items on the invoice, or it can create a separate line on the invoice and post the costs to that line.

The latter option does not pass the costs to the materials, so choose this option if you want that result. The setting is controlled by company code. Figure 4.22 shows the configuration screen.

Figure 4.22 Posting Delivery Costs Configuration Screen

Edit PO Supplement Text in Invoice Verification

Within this option, you can specify whether you want notifiable texts to be displayed during invoice verification and, if so, which texts should trigger the message. See Chapter 2 for details of the functionality. In short, you need to:

1. Select the **Order text general** option to specify the company codes that are relevant to this option.
2. Select the **Notifiable order text types** to specify which purchase order header texts should trigger the message in invoice verification. To do this, you need to add a new entry for the required company code, then double-click the company code and choose the header text types from the options displayed.

Figure 4.23 shows the two main options to be selected.

Figure 4.23 Two Main Options to Control Notifiable Texts

Figure 4.24 shows an example of the notifiable texts.

4.5 Incoming Invoice

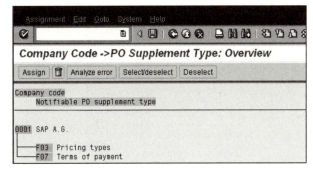

Figure 4.24 Notifiable Texts Screen

Define Mail to Purchasing When Price Variances Occur

This configuration setting can be used to ensure that a message is sent to a user when an invoice price variance occurs. This is sent as an email or SAPmail message depending on how your technical team has set up this kind of communication.

The user informed would normally be the buyer or the person who raised the purchase order. Within this configuration step, you merely decide if a message should be sent. The choice is controlled by a flag for each company code.

In the message-determination configuration, you decide how the system determines to whom and in what format the message is sent.

Configure Vendor-Specific Tolerances

Even though this is called "vendor-specific," you don't actually specify a vendor in the configuration. You specify a tolerance group, and the vendor master record also contains a tolerance group. In effect, these are vendor-tolerance group tolerances. There are two main options:

- A simple tolerance that will post any differences for this group of vendors to a "small differences account" if the differences are within the tolerances specified (i.e., percentage or value and with a negative or positive difference)
- An automatic invoice-reduction tolerance that will cause an automatic credit note to be raised for the difference if it is within the tolerances set. See Section 2.5 for an explanation of invoice reduction.

Set the check-limit flag if you want that specific tolerance to be considered, and enter the tolerance percentage and/or value you want to apply. These settings are controlled by company code and tolerance group. See Figure 4.25 for a sample tolerance configuration.

Maintain Bar-Code Entry

This configuration controls the ability to store a bar code along with the invoice details. You create a new entry for each company code for which you wish to capture bar codes and enter document types that are relevant for bar-code storage. This will trigger an additional window in the invoice verification transaction MIRO where you can input the bar code.

Figure 4.25 Vendor-Specific Tolerance Settings

Activate Direct Posting to G/L Accounts and Material Account

With this configuration option, you can switch on the ability to enter additional lines on the invoice at invoice verification entry, even if the extra line is not contained on the purchase order. Simply flag the required option or options as follows:

4 Configuration

- The **Dir.posting to G/L acct = active** option allows the users to add additional lines to the invoice posting if they refer to a general ledger account.
- The **Dir. Posting to matl = active** option allows usesr to add additional lines to the invoice posting if they refer to material master records.

Leave both flags set off if the invoice verification function is only to be used for entries that relate to purchase order lines. If you want your entry clerks to be able to add additional lines to an invoice within MIRO, then switch the appropriate flag or flags on.

Maintain Item-List Variants
In this option, you specify the layout of the line display in the SAP Invoice Verification main screen. In effect, you are maintaining a type of screen variant with each field available for display. If you wish to change anything, it is best to leave the existing standard layouts as they are and create copies.

Aggregation
The aggregation function in SAP Invoice Verification controls what aggregation of line items occurs. If the invoice total matches the total value of all of the purchase orders keyed against the invoice, the match can be made.

The configuration controls the way that the items can be aggregated. The first step, **Maintain Variants for Aggregation List**, acts in the same way as the **Maintain Item List Variants** does, and the screens look identical although different programs are used.

The second step, **Preset Aggregation Criteria**, is where the controls are entered against the aggregation variant that the settings relate to. You specify the elements of the purchase orders to be aggregated, such as delivery note, material, etc. The detail-configuration screen is shown in Figure 4.26.

Define Start Logo
Although this merely allows you to display a logo on the SAP Invoice Verification screen, it is far more useful than it at first appears.

Many implementations involve multiple company codes. If you set a different logo for each company, this could prevent erroneous entries, and the user would be

Figure 4.26 Detail Screen of Aggregation Configuration

able to spot the difference easily if the wrong company code was specified. Without this logo, it is not easy to see which company code has been defaulted.

You merely flag the company code to switch on the display within transaction MIRO and specify the URL where the logo is stored, normally in a directory on your network.

Set Check for Duplicate Invoices
This configuration controls the check for duplicate entries that is applied to the reference-document number entered at the time of invoice entry. This reference field is normally used to capture the vendor's invoice number. With the check activated, the user will receive a message if the same reference number has already been used on another invoice, because this could indicate that the invoice has already been posted.

You need to indicate whether this check should take place and, if so, what check should be carried out. You achieve this by setting the three flags on the relevant company code line.

The first flag, **Check co. code**, should be set *on* if you want the system to check for the same reference number within the same company code. Set the flag *off* if you want to check for duplicates across all company codes.

The second flag, **Check reference**, controls whether the check should take place at all. Leave this alone if you do not want to check for duplicates. This could be necessary if you are not using the reference field for the vendor's invoice number and as a result duplicates will often occur.

The final flag, **Check inv. Date** should be set *on* if you want to check for duplicate entries on the same date. With this flag set off, duplicates will be allowed as long as they have a different invoice date. This setting could be useful if a vendor sends in invoices with the same reference number, but on different dates.

Nota Fiscal and Chain Liabilities

These are country-specific requirements and will be covered by your SAP documentation for that country's solution.

Prepayment (New to ERP 6)

This functionality covers the process of the prepayment of invoices even though the goods receipt may not have been posted.

Note that if you have used the **GR-Based IV** flag on the PO no prepayment can be posted. This flag indicates that you want to verify invoices against receipts and so prepayment is not an option.

The configuration settings allow the setting of a flag on the vendor that can default into the invoice. This flag can then be used to indicate if advance payment is relevant to each invoice. The flag defaulted from the vendor master can be changed in the invoice entry. This must be the parking of the invoice and not the full invoice process via transaction MIRO.

The configuration also enables the document type to be specified for the prepayment posting.

There are three main steps in the configuration process.

The first step is **Configure Field control for prepayment**.

This is where you can control which fields are open for input after a prepayment invoice has been posted. The default is that all fields are protected from input unless specified in this configuration step. There is a field-status group that can be allocated to each company code and so each company code could have different field control. Select the field-status group that you wish to update and then add the fields that you want to control. If you want to create a new status group, simply enter the four-character code in the work area field when prompted.

Figure 4.27 shows the Field status group window that appears when you enter the configuration step **Configure Field control for prepayment**.

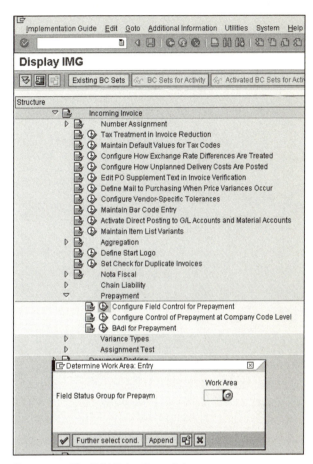

Figure 4.27 The Field Status Group Entry

Once you have specified an existing status group (if you want to change it) or a new status group (if you want to create a new one), you can then indicate which fields should be open for input on the invoice after the prepayment has been posted. If you do not specify a field on this list, the default for that field will be that it will be locked for input. If you specify a field, you will have three options available:

1. You can set the flag to indicate that it should be left as not ready for input. This has the same effect as not specifying the field at all and could be useful if you want to change an existing entry to this setting from a previous setting.

2. You can indicate that the field is to be set to limited changes. This will allow changes to this field, but only

if the same field can be changed on the prepayment document.

3. You can indicate that the field is open for changes regardless of the prepayment field settings. Remember that certain fields on the invoice document will remain unavailable for change even if they are flagged here. The fields may be essential to the process and so may be controlled directly by the program instead of by this entry.

Figure 4.28 shows the three options available for each field.

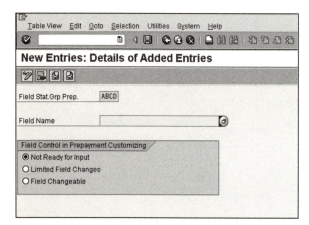

Figure 4.28   Three Options Available for Field Control

The second step in the configuration of prepayments is the **Configure Control of Prepayment at Company Code Level**.

This is where you make the main settings that control the prepayment process. These settings are controlled by company code.

Specify the company code that you wish to configure, and then make the following settings.

- **Doc Type** — Allocates a specific financial document type to the company code. It might be worth creating a new financial document type specifically for prepayment, but you could use an existing document type.
- **Reason** — Allows you to specify a reason for the prepayment. You may need to configure some new reason codes if you wish to use this option. This can be left blank if not required.
- **Field Group** — This is where you allocate the field group used above to the company code.

- **Dist Sys** — Activate this field if you are using distributed systems. The normal setting would be *off* unless you have separate SAP systems in use that communicate with each other technically.
- **Prepay For** — This field is used to indicate which documents are relevant to prepayment. You can leave the field blank, which would mean that parked documents will not be prepaid. You can specify:
  - A — Selected, saved and fully saved documents can be prepaid
  - B — Only saved and fully saved documents can be prepaid
  - C — Only fully saved documents can be prepaid
- **Dis Prf Ctr** — This controls whether the system should post to the correct profit center or a dummy profit center when a prepayment is made. This setting is relevant to the New General Ledger functionality.

Figure 4.29 shows the **Configure Control of Prepayment at Company Code Level** configuration screen.

Figure 4.29   Settings on Configure Control of Prepayment at Company Code Level Screen

The final step is to check the Business Add-In (BAdI) for prepayment options.

This is a step that ideally should be carried out with guidance from your Advanced Business Application Programming (ABAP) resource.

We recommend that you read through the documentation for this step by clicking on the document icon. The information on the help screen explains this fully.

Variance types (New to ERP 6)

Variance types can be helpful when dealing with multi-line invoices. The user can sort the display into variance type sequence and thereby see the potential problem lines at the top of the list.

There are only two standard variance types provided but you can add additional ones and a special BAdI is provided to enable you to determine your own variance types and allocate them to invoice lines depending on the data or circumstances involved.

The first step is the Maintain Variance Types option. In this you will see the two standard SAP variance types, and you can add more as and when you need them. There are just two fields, the key (two characters) and the description of the variance type (50 characters long).

Figure 4.30 shows the variance-types configuration screen with the two SAP standard entries shown.

Figure 4.30 Settings on Variance Types Screen

The second step is to check the BAdI. Change variance types.

Use the help documentation provided for this step to see the methods available for setting the variance type code, depending on formulas or scenarios.

Assignment Test (New to ERP 6)

This functionality is designed to speed up the process of entering bulk invoices via the background.

There may be many millions of POs, goods receipts, and invoices on the system. When posting invoices in bulk, it can take a long time to process because the system searches through these records to find a good match for the invoice. This new functionality checks for activity on the POs that are linked to the invoice. If no activity is found, the system moves on to the next invoice instead of wasting time and effort trying to match the invoice against a PO that has not yet had a receipt or similar activity.

To fine-tune this functionality, you have to set one or more assignment test groups by company code. When creating or amending a vendor, you can then assign the appropriate test group (if any) to that vendor master record and so dictate the settings that should apply.

In the configuration step **Define assignment test group** you configure the settings that will be used for each test group (by company code). The combination of company code and test group allows you to have different settings for groups of vendors and also to have different settings for the same test group in different company codes.

Enter the company code you want to configure and specify a new (or existing) **Assignment test group**. Then enter the settings you require to the following five other fields.

- **Wait time** — Indicates how many days the system should wait before trying to find a match (if no purchase order or delivery is relevant, or if a PO is relevant but the delivery date is not clear.
- **Add to delivery date** — Indicates how many days the system should add to the delivery date of the PO. The assignment will not be attempted until this date has passed. If your vendor normally delivers up to five days later than the requested delivery date, then enter "5" in this field so that the match is not attempted too early.
- **Duration to check** — Can be used to enter the number of days that the system should wait regardless of the PO dates. Service-entry sheets have a complicated allocation process (it is not a simple GR process). Use this delay for the test group that you assign to your service-only related vendors.
- **Interval Btw 2 Assignment Tests** — Is used to determine how many days the system should wait after an unsuccessful assignment, before trying to assign again. Use a low number if your processing times are not excessive and then increase this number if the run is taking too long.
- **Max Assignment Test Period** — Indicates when the assignment test should stop. If the system has been trying to assign a match for a long period, it could be that the assignment will never occur. Use a large number so that items are not left out of the test too early, then reduce this period if you have an increasing number of documents that stay unassigned for long periods.

Figure 4.31 shows the **Assignment test groups** configuration screen.

4 Configuration

Figure 4.31 Settings on Assignment Test Groups Screen

4.6 Document Parking

You only need to configure document parking settings if you want to block parked invoices from further processing, depending on the value of the invoice.

If you do want to use this functionality, the configuration step should only be completed by an experienced workflow consultant. The workflow template for document completion and the template for release for posting are technical configuration steps that require workflow expertise. The help documentation covers the basic details. Consult your workflow specialist for how this should be configured.

The definition of the release criteria, however, is not complicated. The configuration controls those invoices that are parked. It prevents them from being fully posted until they have been released by an authorized user.

The **Define Release Criteria** step allows you to set up an authorization process. You specify the company code that is to be controlled and specify the person or function that is to be responsible for the release of the document. You can have many entries with different value levels. If the document has a value below the limit, it is not blocked. If it is above this limit, then it is blocked for posting and — depending on the value — it will be allocated to a specified user. Figure 4.32 shows the **Define Release Criteria** configuration screen.

Figure 4.32 Release Criteria Configuration Screen

4.7 Invoice Block

In this phase of the configuration you will set up the payment blocks and how they are used. Payment blocks are needed to prevent invoices from being paid because of mismatches or to block matched invoices for payment in disputes and other special situations.

The main tolerances are controlled here. Remember that invoice tolerances don't stop the invoice from being posted; they merely indicate whether the payment block should be set. If the payment block is applied to an invoice, it will behave exactly like an invoice that has not been blocked, but the payment run will not automatically pay the vendor. All financial postings and all other updates still take place even though there is a mismatch.

Determine Payment Block

All that you need to do in this step is to configure any additional payment blocks that you need. The user could enter manual blocks during invoice verification. You can only change the descriptions of the main blocks, as no other settings are controlled here. Normally, you do not need to do anything in this step.

Set Tolerance Limits

This is a very important step and should be carried out with the full involvement of the financial department. This configuration will control the situations where an exact match cannot be determined. The difference between the amount due to the vendor and the value of the invoice can be allowed, and so can result in overpayments. It is therefore vital that tolerances are fully agreed upon by all interested parties before invoices are posted for the first time.

The settings will be used to block invoices that exceed the set tolerances and prevent the automatic payment. There are no recommended tolerance levels. The levels used depend on many different factors, the most important of which is the actual cost of investigating discrepancies.

If the cost of investigating a mismatch is very low, then you can set your tolerances to be reasonably strict. If the cost of investigating mismatches is high, then you should consider being slightly more lenient.

For example, the time involved can be significant if you take into consideration the time taken to post the invoice initially (longer because of the mismatch), the time taken to pass on the invoice for investigation, the actual time during the investigation (including telephone calls and letters), plus the time taken to finally clear the mismatch.

Let's assume for this example that the cost is approximately € 50. If you have set the tolerance value to block invoices where the vendor has overcharged you by more than € 10, then you will effectively spend € 50 to regain € 10. Naturally, if the vendor was to find out that you have a tolerance of € 50, and this vendor was not thoroughly honest, it could ensure that it always overcharged by € 49. Therefore, you have to choose sensible levels that are low enough to trap overcharges but not so low that you are spending more on matching than the overcharges you are trapping.

If you are setting up a new company code in your development system, copying the tolerances shown in Figure 4.33 from Company Code 0001 will at least enable you to raise invoices. You can then adjust the settings as you learn the precise tolerances you require.

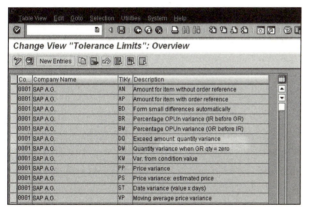

Figure 4.33 Basic Set of Tolerances

The main tolerances all have upper and lower limits for percentage and value. The value is in the default currency of the company code. You also have flags that indicate that the tolerance should be checked. Figure 4.34 shows a typical tolerance with all of the settings available.

The following tolerances are the most common:

- **AN** (amount for item without order reference) — This tolerance is used when a line has been added to the invoice that does not reference a purchase order or similar document. Use this tolerance to block invoices with

Figure 4.34 Typical Invoice Tolerance Screen

manual entries. The tolerance limit is normally quite high because your own clerks have entered this data.

- **AP** (amount for item with order reference) — This tolerance is used if you wish to block invoice lines that exceed a certain value even if they fully match against a referenced document. This is normally set very high and is often seen as a block that is used as a comfort factor, so that large invoice values can be checked. Often this tolerance value is increased after a short period when it becomes clear that the system is operating correctly and capturing erroneous invoices automatically.

- **BD** (form small differences automatically) — Use extreme caution with this tolerance. It should be set very low: € 0.05 or less. It is designed to manage rounding errors, typically caused by tax calculations. It is unique in that it does not set the blocking flag on the invoice but merely allows a tolerance when the mathematical check is carried out to ensure that the invoice value equates to the data entered.

- **BR** and **BW** (percentage OPUn variance with IR before GR and Percentage OPUn variance with GR before IR) — This is a tolerance that checks the order price unit variances. An example of the order price unit is where you may purchase one barrel of a fluid and the price is € 50 a barrel and the barrel is to contain 50 liters. If the receipt is for one barrel, but there are only 40 liters in the barrel, then the order price has varied. This tolerance allows the vendor some leeway when it comes to invoices for items that fall onto this category where the contents can vary under normal circumstances.

- **DQ** (exceed amount: quantity variance) — This tolerance controls quantity variances. If you purchase bulk materials, the actual quantities can vary, and so you may wish to allow some tolerance on invoices. If you only purchase items that have specific quantities, you may wish to set this tolerance to zero. Even though this is a quantity variance, the system takes the value of the item into consideration. In this way, a small quantity discrepancy on an expensive item may be blocked, but a larger discrepancy on a lower-priced item may be allowed.

- **DW** (Quantity variance when GR qty = zero) — The system will use the PO price to calculate the value of the item, as opposed to the goods-receipt value used in the previous tolerance. If you don't maintain this tolerance for your company code, the system will block an invoice for which no goods receipt has been posted. If you want to allow the posting of such an invoice, set the tolerance limits for this tolerance to **Do not check**.

- **KW** (variance from condition value) — This tolerance focuses on the planned delivery costs and will block an invoice if the invoiced planned delivery cost varies from the value stored with the condition type used on the conditions on the purchase order.

- **LA** (amount of blanket purchase order) — The system will check the total invoiced value for the blanket purchase order plus this invoice against the value limits specified in the order. The tolerances will dictate if the invoice should be blocked.

- **LD** (blanket purchase order time limit exceeded) — This compares the invoice date against the allowed invoice interval on the purchase order and blocks the invoice if the tolerance has been exceeded.

- **PP** (price variance) — This can be set to allow small price variances. The lower limit and percentage would appear to be unnecessary, so why would you want to block an invoice for payment simply because the vendor has undercharged you? The answer is that you probably wouldn't, but if the difference is high then perhaps there has been a keying error or a vendor error, and so it would be worth verifying the facts before making the payment. We recommend setting a relatively high lower tolerance for underpayments.

- **PS** (price variance — estimated price) — This is another hidden gem that is often overlooked even though it can be very useful. There are often certain vendors or certain purchase orders for which the price is almost always wrong because you do not always know when the purchase order is raised. There may be further actions after ordering that affect the price, for instance. If this is the case, you can flag the price as an estimated price in the PO condition control tab (seen in Figure 4.35). This will ensure that the estimated price tolerance is checked instead of the normal price-variance tolerance. This flag is ideal in situations where you have variable prices but there is an element of trust with the vendor used.

- **ST** (date variance — value X days) — This tolerance is actually a number of days multiplied by the invoice value. It is used to prevent the early payment to a vendor when it has delivered the goods early and sent the invoice before the delivery date has been reached. Multiplying the value by the number of days early (i.e., invoice date compared to the delivery date on the purchase order) gives the figure that is checked against the tolerance. This means that an item 100 days early valued at € 10 will be treated the same as an item one day early with a value of € 1,000.

Figure 4.35 Estimated Price Flag

▶ **VP** (moving average price variance) — This tolerance does not affect the invoice block, but instead is used to warn the user that the invoice posting will affect the MAP by an amount that exceeds the tolerance. This is an important setting, because if an invoice price is different from the MAP it will alter that MAP, even if the invoice is blocked for payment. This would normally trigger a warning message — allowing the user to continue — but the message can be set to an error if you want to prevent the corruption of the MAP, a topic covered in Chapter 3.

Activate Workflow Template

This is where your workflow consultant will configure the templates that would be used if you are using workflow messages when item lines are blocked via transaction MIRO. The message and the associated processing can be managed via this step.

Typically, if an invoice is blocked because the price does not match the PO, a workflow message can be sent to the buyer (or PO creator, or requisitioner) asking them to check the details and action any errors (by changing the price if appropriate) from within that workflow message. Similarly, if the quantity on the invoice is greater than the quantity on the PO, the workflow message can be sent to the person responsible for posting the goods receipt and he can post further receipts via the workflow message if this is appropriate.

Item Amount Check

This is not actually a tolerance, but rather a setting that will communicate to the system whether the item value should be checked against the **AP** and **AN** tolerances described above.

You can first indicate if the check should be carried out, using the **Activate Amount Check** configuration. You merely flag the company codes that you want to use for the check. In the **Set Item Amount Check** field, you specify the type of order line to be checked.

One use for this setting is to block all items that have the GR flag set *off*. With this flag off, there is no three-way matching because the flag indicates whether a goods receipt is necessary. Without a goods receipt, there is nothing to check at the invoice stage relating to quantity.

In this case you can set the item amount check to be triggered if the item has the GR flag off. You can also specify the item category if required, so that you can carry out the tolerance check on special purchase orders such as a sub-contract.

Figure 4.36 shows an example of a setting in which the system will check all purchase order lines where the GR flag is off. Here, all purchase orders share a standard item category.

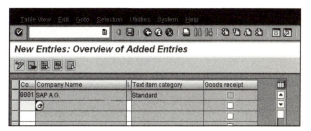

Figure 4.36 Set-Item-Amount Check Screen

Stochastic Blocks

A stochastic block is effectively a random block. It is designed to block a portion of invoices that normally would not have been blocked. It is also designed to be used as a type of spot check. It can be quite scary to have all invoices automatically paid if they match. This is especially true when SAP is being used for the first time in a company. This check can be used to increase confidence in the automatic matching process. The invoices blocked in this way can be selected when using the MRBR transaction, so that they can be subject to a second manual check. Figure 4.37 shows the flag that can be set on transaction MRBR to show invoices that have been stochastically blocked.

The first step is to use the **Activate Stochastic Block** function to flag the company codes that you want to take part in the check. The second step is to use the **Set Stochastic Block** function to set the parameters. There are two parameters: the **Threshold value** and the **Percentage**.

Set the **Percentage** as the percentage of invoices that you want to be randomly blocked. Every invoice equal to or greater than the **Threshold value** will be considered relevant, and the specified percentage of these invoices will be blocked. Invoices below this value will still be considered by the stochastic check, but as the value reduces so does the chance of them being stochastically blocked.

4 Configuration

Figure 4.37 Stochastic Block Flag on the MRBR Transaction

In this manner, an invoice with a value of half of the threshold is half as likely to be blocked as an invoice that is equal to or greater than the threshold value. The threshold thus is not value above which the invoices will be stochastically blocked. It is, rather, a ceiling for the percentage above which the percentage likelihood of the invoice being blocked stays the same but below which the likelihood decreases proportionately.

4.8 Clearing Account Maintenance

This configuration step simply controls the number ranges that relate to the clearing accounts for GR/IR, freight, and customs postings.

4.9 Invoice Verification in Background

This configuration step, **Define Automatic Status Change**, allows you to set a flag that will change the status of an invoice if it has been verified in the background. Remember to keep the following in mind:

- Set the flag *on* if you want the matched invoices to have the status set so that they can be identified as being correct but not complete.
- Set the flag set *off* if you want invoices posted in the background will appear as completed and so will appear identical to those manually posted.

4.10 Electronic Data Interchange (EDI)

If you accept invoices via EDI, you can use these settings to convert the data on the EDI record to the correct data used in your system. Tax codes and company codes can be converted. The third step allows you to make various settings that indicate how the invoice data should be processed. These settings indicate which invoice document type should be used, whether the documents should be parked or fully posted, and which checks should be carried out. Figure 4.38 shows the settings that can be made in the third step: **Enter Program Parameters**.

Figure 4.38 Available Program Parameters

4.11 Evaluated Release Settlement (ERS)

This step is new to ERP 6. It covers the configuration of the ERS for planned delivery costs and the use of number ranges specific to ERS invoices.

Specify Automatic Settlement of Planned Delivery Costs (New to ERP 6)

The step allows you to indicate which vendors should be included in the ERS for planned delivery costs. The settings are controlled by company code and purchasing organization and so you can have different settings for different combinations. You may need to have many different entries for each vendor, especially if you have many company codes and purchasing organizations. This may seem obvious, but you have to remember that every combination of the two would need to be specified if you want all planned delivery cists for the vendor to be settled via ERS. Blanks are not allowed for any entry; each field on the configuration table (apart from the flag) is mandatory.

ERS Invoice Numbering (New to ERP 6)
In certain countries (currently France, Hungary, and Spain) the law dictates that ERS invoices have to have fully sequential numbering for each vendor (i.e., without gaps). You cannot therefore use the standard functionality, because the invoice numbering will be sequential within the company code, but not within the vendor.
SAP has provided the configuration options to enable these laws to be met.

You create ERS Number groups (in the steps detailed below) and then specify the relevant number group on each vendor master record that will use the ERS process. The group is specified in the **Tax Number 4** field, on the **Control** screen for that vendor. This will ensure that the correct number range is used and that the numbers will be sequential for that vendor.

- **Create number groups** is the step used to simply create a group and give it a text description.
- **Assign ERS Number Ranges to Company Codes** takes you to the same configuration step as when you use the SPRO menu option **Financial accounting > Enter Global Parameters configuration**. Here you must click on the **additional details** function and enter the two-character number range code that you will use for that company code. This would allocate a set number range to the company code.
- **Create ERS Invoice Number Ranges** is the step where you allocate the number range code to the ERS number-range group. You then specify the number range you want for that number range code in the same way that you manage and create number ranges elsewhere in SAP.

This step is required if you want to then allocate the ERS number group to a specific vendor or vendors.

4.12 Message Determination

This step controls the output, printing, emails, etc. of any messages or documents. This is the standard SAP method of using the condition technique to control the output.

4.13 Define Document Life

In this step, you define the number of days that a fully processed invoice should remain in the system before it is considered by the archiving run.

4.14 Authorization Management

In this step, your authorization consultant can manage the authorization profiles and maintain the authorizations, but there is a step that can be used to control the limits of groups of users. This is controlled by the use of tolerance groups. If you assign users to tolerance groups, you can then limit these groups by company code. The limits you can control are:
- The total value per document
- The value per open account item
- The maximum cash discount that can be used
- A set of permitted payment differences

4.15 Maintain Customer Exits and Business Add-Ins

In this step, your technical team can manage any user exits that are required. See Section 1.17 for a full list of the BAdIs that are available for invoice verification.

4.16 Logistics Invoice Verification: Index

This is not actually a configuration step. It provides instructions on how to use the index on the invoice verification documents. Unless you have a very small quantity of invoices, switching on this index will speed up bulk processing and reports. There will be additional overhead on the creation of new documents (because the index is maintained online), but this overhead should almost be invisible.

4.17 Business Add-Ins and User Exits in Invoice Verification (New to ERP 6)

There are many BAdIs available and this list shows the relevant BAdI and a short description of its use. Your ABAP consultant will be able to use these to enhance the functionality available or "personalize" the SAP function to match your requirements.

Even though these options are provided by SAP, you should still only use them if you have no alternative. A fully standard SAP function is more likely to present you with fewer technical problems and is more likely to provide you with a fully robust process. Having noted that, an implementation rarely fully avoids the use of BAdIs and user exits and so it is likely that you will at least need to know of their existence and use.

- **MRM_HEADER_DEFAULT** to pre-assign various header fields
- **MRM_PAYMENT_TERMS** to set terms of payment
- **MRM_UDC_DISTRIBUTE** to distribute unplanned delivery costs
- **MRM_TRANSACT_DEFAULT** to pre-assign various transaction fields
- **MRM_WT_SPLIT_UPDATE** to change the withholding tax data and the data for a vendor split
- **MRM_TOLERANCE_GROUP** to set vendor-specific tolerance groups
- **MRM_RELEASE_CHECK** for additional checks before invoices are released; i.e., you can restrict the list of invoices to be released by defining your own criteria
- **MRM_MRIS_HDAT_MODIFY** to change header data for invoicing plan settlement
- **MRM_MRIS_IDAT_MODIFY** to change item data for invoicing plan settlement
- **MRM_MRKO_HDAT_MODIFY** to change the document header data for consignment settlement
- **MRM_ITEM_CUSTFIELDS** to change customers' own fields
- **ParkFromData**
  - **BAPI_INCOMINGINVOICE_PARK**: Park invoice
- **SaveFromData**
  - **BAPI_INCOMINGINVOICE_SAVE**: Enter invoice for verification in the background
- **PreliminaryPostSingle**
  - **BAPI_INCOMINGINVOICE_POST**: Post provisional invoice
- **DeleteSingle**
  - **BAPI_INCOMINGINVOICE_DELETE**: Delete provisional invoice
- **Change**
  - **BAPI_INCOMINGINVOICE_CHANGE**: Change provisional invoice

You can use a customer enhancement to help you post to material or general ledger accounts during processing of invoices incoming via EDI using Logistics Invoice Verification. To do this, use the enhancement MRMH0002 with the user exit: EXIT_SAPLMRMH_015.

Changes to Existing User Exits and Includes in Latest Releases

The include **RMMR1MI1** that was used as a replacement for the customer exit in automatic invoicing plan settlement (MRIS) has been deleted as of SAP R/3 Enterprise core 4.70 (SAP_APPL 470). To change header and item data in invoicing plan settlement, you should now use the BAdI **MRM_MRIS_HDAT_MODIFY** (change header data for invoicing plan settlement), or the BAdI **MRM_MRIS_IDAT_MODIFY** (change item data for invoicing plan settlement).

The customer exit **EXIT_RMVKON00_003** and **EXIT_RMVKON90_001** (customer exit for conventional invoice verification) for consignment and pipeline settlement (MRKO) was deleted as of SAP R/3 Enterprise core 4.70 (SAP_APPL 470). To change the vendor and document type in consignment settlement, you should now use the BAdI **MRM_MRKO_HDAT_MODIFY**. Note that when you switch from consignment settlement in conventional invoice verification to Logistics Invoice Verification, all documents must have been settled using the customer exit **EXIT_RMVKON90_001**.

4.18 Summary

In this chapter, the configuration of SAP Invoice Verification was discussed. Remember that the SAP help available within configuration will also help explain the options available.

Our own style of configuration is to use the options available to the full, and this often results in fewer user exits and or modifications.

We firmly believe that the standard SAP invoice verification functionality is so rich (especially with the use of the many configuration options) that you should not have to employ any user exits or modifications. If you believe that you do need to use these, then please make sure that you are not changing the system to match the business process when a change to the process may, in the long run, lead to a better system altogether.

Index

A

ABAP 17
account assignment 65, 66
account assignment category 24
account check 69
account configuration 68
account modifier 68, 69
account numbers 65
accounting documents 70
accounting processes 65
accounting view 55, 69
actual payment date 71
additional charges 28, 40
additional invoice 28
additional lines on the invoice 73
additional Log 58
aggregation 74
allocations 24
allowed invoice interval on the purchase order 80
Amount 11, 55
amount field 39
amount for item with order reference 79
amount for item without order reference 79
amount of blanket purchase order 80
Application area 69
archiving 83
authorization 83
authorized 30
authorizing the payment 11
automatic account determination 25, 35, 49, 65
automatic clearance 53
automatic credit note 71, 73
automatic date calculations 39
automatic invoice reduction tolerance 73
automatic invoice release 14
automatic payment 78
automatic postings 35
automatic release 21

B

BACS 57
balances 27
bar Code 73
basic data 11
Basic data tab 35, 54
batch job 21
batch runs 63
bill-of-lading 21
blanket purchase order time limit exceeded 80
block 23, 29, 30, 33, 79
block parked invoices 78
blocked 10, 11, 21, 27, 28, 29, 31, 32, 33, 51, 78
blocked for payment 10, 20
blocked invoices 12, 13, 14
blocking flags 12, 49
blocking of invoices for payment 70
blocking reasons 14
BOMs 36
bulk materials 53

C

calculate tax 55
Calculate tax flag 39, 55
calculate taxes automatically 71
cash discounts 71
cash-flow 29
chart of accounts 67, 69
check for Duplicate Invoices 74
check of Referenced G/L Accounts 69
check-limit flag 73
city 65
clear manually 53
clearing account 35, 50, 52, 53, 82
clearing document 54
company code 28, 30, 54, 57, 65, 69, 70, 71, 72, 73, 74, 78, 79, 81, 82, 83
complaint document 71
complex invoice 15
condition types 25, 26
Configure Automatic Postings 62
consignment stocks 35
correction ID 33
credit note 10, 33, 35, 39, 40, 51, 71
credits 67
Customs 24, 49

D

date variance 80
dates 29
deadlines 58
Debit/Credit 67, 68
debits 67
default codes 54
default tax codes 71
Define Attributes of System Messages 61
define tax jurisdiction 64
delivery 21, 22, 23, 26
  charges 24, 25, 26, 27, 28, 40
  costs 27, 56
  date 29, 80
  note 19, 20, 21, 74
  surplus 52
  tab 38
different tax codes 55
Direct Posting to G/L Accounts and Material Account 73
discounts 58
document types 70, 73, 82

E

early payment to a vendor 80
EDI 82
email 13, 17, 73
error-message 30, 62
ERS 21, 31, 35, 36, 52, 54
exceed amount, quantity variance 80

Index

exchange rate 58
exchange rate differences 72
exchange rate table 72
exclude items due for payment 58
exclude values 58

F

F110 57, 59
F110S 57, 59
FBL1N 13
Financial Accounting menu 61
financial postings 49, 53
form small differences automatically 30, 79
free Selection 58
freight 24, 49, 52
freight provisions 65
full payment run 59

G

G/L account 65, 68, 69
G/L account number 66, 68
gas, electricity, or water 36
general ledger 49, 65
general modification 68
general-ledger account 35, 49, 69
goods receipt 10, 13, 14, 19, 20, 21, 22, 26, 31, 51
goods receipt/invoice receipt (GR/IR) clearing 28, 50, 65
goods receipt-based invoice verification 15
goods-receipt 17, 26, 32, 35, 39, 55, 57, 69
goods-receipt flag 38
goods-receipt/invoice-receipt clearing account 49
goods-receipt-based invoice verification 19
GR (Goods Receipt) flag 81
GR based IV flag 21, 22
GR flag 39
GR/IR clearing account 50, 51, 54, 68
GR-based IV flag 20, 23, 50
group similar plants 65

H

Handling Mismatched Invoices 11
header conditions 26
header delivery costs 26
header text 42
header text types 72
help-text 61

I

identification code 57
IMG 61
IMG Projects 61
Info Record 23, 31, 35, 36
input mode 69
input of material number 69
input of valuation class 69
insurance 24
inter-or intra-company purchases 31
invoice
    overview 15
    quantity 29
    reduction 33, 71, 73
    surplus 52
    tab 38, 54
    tolerances 11
    value 31
    Verification text 41
Invoice amount acc. to vendor 34
Invoice qty acc. to vendor 34
invoice-relevant notes 41
invoices posted in the background 82
invoicing plan 38
item category 81
item conditions 26
item List Variants 74
item text 41

L

last movement before key date 53
layout of the line display 74
leases 37
liability account 35
line items 11
Logistics Invoice Verification 61

M

Maintain Number Assignments for Accounting Documents 70
Maintain Variants for Aggregation List 74
manage small differences 55
manage small differences tolerance 11
MAP 29, 33, 35, 40, 54, 56, 57, 62, 69, 81
matched invoice 49
material 24, 74
material document 22
material master 55
material master record (Accounting View) 24, 65
material price 24
material types 65
materials-management postings 49
maximum cah discount 83
memos 41
Message Determination 83
message number 63
message-determination configuration 73
messages 62
MIGO 22, 26
MIR6 15
MIR7 15
MIRO 7, 8, 11, 32, 54
mismatch 13, 33, 78
mismatched invoices 10, 16
modifications 85
movement type 68
moving average price 27
Moving average price variance 81
Moving average variance 29
MR11 51, 53
MRBR 8, 10, 13, 21, 33, 81
MRIS 37, 39
MRKO 36
MRRL 32
multiple companies 57
multiple company codes 74
multiple tax codes 55

N

net 55
net price 38
Net proposal 55
next payment run 58
No ERS flag 32

Index

non-invoiced receipts 50, 52
non-valuated receipt 38
notifiable text window 41
notifiable texts 42, 72
number ranges 70

O

open account item 83
open item 36
Options 68
output type 32
overcharge 33, 55, 79
overpaid 20, 31
overpayments 78

P

paid on time 20
parameter tab 57
park 20, 23
parked 21, 82
Parking 15
partial delivery 50
partial payments 37
payment 27, 29, 49
   block 78
   differences 83
   logs 58
   methods 57
   run 32, 57, 58, 71
   run date 57
   schedule 38
   terms 31, 32, 71
Percentage OPUn variance with IR before GR 79
periodic invoice plans 39
pipeline liabilities 36
pipeline materials 35, 36
planned delivery charges 24, 25, 28
planned delivery cost 80
plant 17, 64, 65, 66, 68, 69
posting date 32
postings 49
price calculation schema 26
price control 55
price differences 55
price variance 40, 49, 65, 72, 73, 80
price variance account 35, 54, 56, 57
price variance, estimated price 80
prices 29

pricing conditions 24
pricing scales 26
print program 59
printout/data medium 59
profit and loss 56
proposal flag 59
proposal run 59
proposed payments 59
purchase order 10, 11, 14, 17, 19, 21, 23, 25, 27, 28, 30, 31, 35, 36, 41, 54
purchase order header 40, 41
purchase order header text 41
purchase order history 40
purchase order price 20
purchase order reference 41
purchase prices 56
purchasing configuration 26
purchasing data 32
purchasing group 14

Q

Qty Var. Less Than/Equal To 53
quantity 23
quantity invoiced 50
quantity received 31, 50
quantity variance 17, 21
quantity variance when GR qty = zero 80

R

random block 81
rate type M 58
RE 70
receipt 24, 49
reference 57
reference document 22
reference document number 74
regular payments 37
release automatically 14
release invoices 10, 14
released 23
rentals 37
requisitioner 17
RN (net) 70, 71
rounding 11
rounding errors 11, 30, 55
royalty and license payments 36
rules 67, 68
rules of accounting 65

S

SAP help 85
SAP Reference Implementation Guide 61
SAPmail 13, 17, 73
scanning 10
schedule the payment run 57
scheduling the payment run as a batch job 59
self-billing 21, 35, 39
Set Item Amount Check 81
set value payments 37
settlement program 32, 35
simulate postings 68
simulation 65, 68, 69
small differences 11, 29
small differences account 73
small variances 52
spot check 81
SPRO 61
staged payments 37
stages 37
standard accounts postings 49
standard messages 63
standard price 54, 56, 69
Start Logo 74
status 82
status screen 59
status tab 59
stochastic block 81
stock account 24, 27, 28, 35, 40, 49, 50, 51, 53, 56, 57
storage location 17
subsequent credit 39
subsequent debit 28, 39, 40
summarized invoices 19
summary reports 59
switching off a message 62

T

tax 21, 30, 35, 54, 71
tax accounts 49
tax amount 55
tax calculations 11
tax code 54, 55, 71, 82
Tax Jurisdiction 62
tax procedures 54
taxes 11, 30
test mode 39
test runs 58
text element 41

Index

the cost of investigating mismatches 78
the index on the invoice verification documents 84
three-way matching 19, 20, 21, 24, 27, 28, 31
tolerance 29, 30
tolerance group 73, 83
tolerance keys 30
tolerance limits 78
tolerance percentage and/or value 73
tolerances 11, 23, 28, 29, 73, 78
too early 29
total value 20
traffic light 9
transaction event key 35
transaction/event key 66, 67, 68, 69

U

undercharged 55
unmatched invoice 49
unplanned delivery charges 28, 29, 40
unplanned delivery costs 24, 71, 72
upper and lower limits for percentage and value 79
user exits 83, 85

V

valuation area group 65, 66, 68, 69, 70
valuation class 65, 66, 68, 69
valuation modifier 65, 68
value only credit 40
value only invoice 40
Value Variance Less Than/= To 53
Var. from condition value 80
variances 27
VAT 30, 32
VAT code 54
vendor 14
vendor account 36, 49, 50
vendor master record 31, 73
vendors invoice number 74
Vendor-Specific Tolerances 73
Vendor-Tolerance Group 73

W

warning message 29, 62
workflow 13, 16, 17
write-offs 49
WRX 68

ISBN 978-1-59229-186-1
2nd edition 2008
© 2008 by Galileo Press GmbH
SAP PRESS is an imprint of Galileo Press,
Boston (MA), USA
Bonn, Germany

Editor Stephen Solomon
Copy Editor John Parker
Cover Design Vera Brauner
Production Iris Warkus
Printed in Germany

All rights reserved. Neither this publication nor any part of it may be copied or reproduced in any form or by any means or translated into another language, without the prior consent of Galileo Press Inc., 100 Grossman Drive, Suite 205, Braintree, MA 02184, USA

Galileo Press makes no warranties or representations with respect to the content hereof and specifically disclaims any implied warranties of merchantability or fitness for any particular purpose. Galileo Press assumes no reponsibility for any errors that may appear in this publication.

All of the screenshots and graphics reproduced in this book are subject to copyright © SAP AG, Dietmar-Hopp-Allee 16, 69190 Walldorf, Germany.

SAP, the SAP-Logo, mySAP, SAP NetWeaver, SAP Business Suite, mySAP.com, SAP R/3, SAP R/2, SAP B2B, SAPtronic, SAPscript, SAP BW, SAP CRM, SAP EarlyWatch, SAP ArchiveLink, SAP GUI, SAP Business Workflow, SAP Business Engineer, SAP Business Navigator, SAP Business Framework, SAP Business Information Warehouse, SAP inter-enterprise solutions, SAP APO, AcceleratedSAP, InterSAP, SAPoffice, SAPfind, SAPfile, SAPtime, SAPmail, SAPaccess, SAP-EDI, R/3 Retail, Accelerated HR, Accelerated HiTech, Accelerated Consumer Products, ABAP, ABAP/4, ALE/WEB, BAPI, Business Framework, BW Explorer, Enjoy-SAP, mySAP.com e-business platform, mySAP Enterprise Portals, RIVA, SAPPHIRE, TeamSAP, Webflow and SAP PRESS are registered or unregistered trademarks of SAP AG, Walldorf.

All other products mentioned in this book are registered or unregistered trademarks of their respective companies.